Retiring in Arizona

Retiring in Arizona

Your One-Stop Guide to Living, Loving and Lounging Under the Sun

by Dorothy Tegeler

Third Revised Edition

Published by: Gem Guides Book Company
315 Cloverleaf Drive, Suite F
Baldwin Park, CA 91706
(818)855-1611

© Copyright 1994 Dorothy Tegeler

Cover Design: Michael Stansbury

ISBN 0-935182-69-1

Contents

Illustrations

Acknowledgements

While this book is primarily the work of one author, the contributions of many individuals were essential in its creation. Paul and Laura Geisler get special acclaim for adapting to a "writer's lifestyle." Their patience, assistance and tolerance is greatly appreciated.

Hundreds of individuals have contributed to this book in small, yet significant ways, providing facts and figures, previewing copy and verifying phone numbers.

Introduction

Irresistible, inviting, enticing, magnetic, addictive, and oh, so tempting—ARIZONA!

Visitors under the influence of these sunny skies have sold their homes, packed their bags and set out to pioneer a new lifestyle. They had discovered sunshine—Arizona's golden resource. Add to that low humidity, year-round outdoor activity and friendly folks and you have the land of your dreams.

Whether you're just visiting, have recently moved to the state or are dreaming of the day when you can call Arizona home, this book is for you.

Retiring in Arizona is a compendium of information that will tell you who, what, where, why and how Arizona operates. You'll find facts and figures, anecdotes, directions, history, advice and community resources that will give you that "native edge" in no time.

The book is divided into sections that get you acquainted with the state, give you an in-depth look at more than 40 communities, give advice on finding a place, and actually getting moved and settled. If you're interested in working or starting a business, you'll find valuable information on how to proceed. There are community resources and just for the fun of it—a small introduction to the vast recreational opportunities Arizona serves on a silver platter to residents and visitors alike.

Considerable effort was made to ensure that the information in this book is accurate. Telephone numbers and addresses listed were checked and double-checked before the book went to press, but things change quickly. Check with the Arizona information operators (area code 602) to locate new numbers if you need assistance.

Although Arizona has long been considered a retirement state, less than two percent of the nation's elderly live here. Arizona's not a haven for old folks, but a dynamic state that recognizes and respects the continuing contribution of the American retiree. Our retirees are ageless. Retirees can be in their twenties or their nineties—it's up to you! Arizona's retirees are generally better off financially than retirees in other states and are younger and much more active than their counterparts elsewhere. There are any number of people active in the work force who will tell you they "retired to Arizona" years ago. For many, life in the heart of the Arizona playground is one wonderful day after another. They just happen to work for a living!

As you read this, the next edition of *Retiring in Arizona* is being planned. Won't you help by letting us know of any changes you've encountered since this edition went to press? We'd also like to hear your comments on what you found helpful or wished was included in the book. Send information to the author in care of:

Gem Guides Book Company
315 Cloverleaf Drive, Suite F
Baldwin Park, California 91706

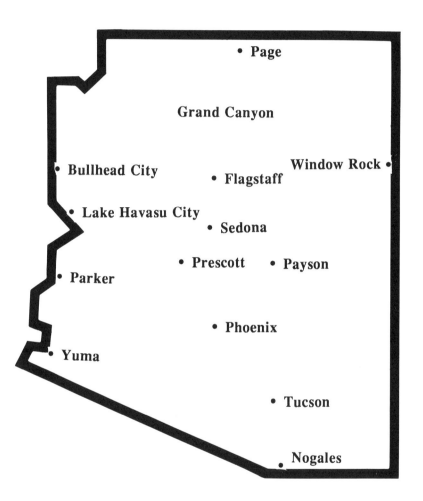

• Page

Grand Canyon

Window Rock •

• Bullhead City

• Flagstaff

• Lake Havasu City

• Sedona

• Prescott   • Payson

• Parker

• Phoenix

• Yuma

• Tucson

Nogales
•

Arizona

Welcome to Arizona

Retirees seeking sun, fun, and good health have been coming to Arizona for decades. The state has been luring new residents from all parts of the United States since the early 1950s. Today, more than three and a half million people call Arizona home, an eightfold increase from 1930 when the state's population was a sparse 438,000.

To many newcomers, Arizona is the land of opportunity. You'll find a pioneering spirit among the state's residents. Many consider the state one of the few remaining frontiers where the enterprising have a chance to make their fortune and retirees can enjoy a carefree active lifestyle.

Shivering Northerners and Midwesterners make up the bulk of the transplants, most of whom arrived declaring that they've shoveled their last snow-filled driveway and listened to the wind chill report for the final time.

Newcomers searching for a small-town environment in the midst of some of the world's most majestic natural backdrops opt for the four-season northern regions where Prescott,

Payson, Flagstaff, and Sedona beckon. Those who come seeking sunshine and warm air choose the state's southern areas, where 85 percent of the population resides. Phoenix, Tucson, and Yuma are major southern Arizona hot spots attracting new residents. Bullhead City, Kingman and Lake Havasu City on the western edge of the state have also become areas of rapid growth.

The Internal Revenue Service reports that more people move to Arizona from California than from any other state, more than twice the number as from Illinois, the next largest contributor of new residents.

With so many new residents, many of whom have left relatives and friends in other parts of the country, it doesn't take long to make new friends. In most communities there are plenty of activities to help you get acquainted.

Over the years, many well-known personalities have chosen to call Arizona home. The roster of Arizona retirees has included celebrities as well as just ordinary folks. Very few Arizona retirees come with a rocking chair, for most retirees Arizona is just a change of scene while continuing to maintain busy schedules.

Retirement Mecca

National recognition of the state as a retirement mecca began in 1954 when Youngtown became the country's first planned retirement community. Youngtown Land and Development Company sold the first home on October 1, 1954.

Six years later, the Del E. Webb Corporation opened the doors at Sun City, the largest adult community in the United States. Today it is home to nearly 40,000 residents. Its sister community, Sun City West, has a population of more than 17,000. A third Del E. Webb community, Sun City Vistoso, opened near Tucson in 1987.

Home States of Arizona Newcomers

California 28,209
Illinois 10,867
New Mexico 10,807
Texas 10,785
Colorado 9,965
Ohio 6,303
Michigan 6,082
Utah 5,471
New York 5,066
Washington 4,932

Source: IRS data matched to census data.

Plans for Sun City got under way in the late 1950s when Del E. Webb bought 8,900 acres of farmland, spent $2 million building five model homes, a shopping center, and other recreational facilities and began promoting the community as an "Active Way of Life!" for those over 50. When Sun City opened in 1960, buyers could put $500 down to purchase a home. The average purchase price was $11,000. Today those same homes are selling for five to six times the original price.

Sun City's opening ushered in a new era inviting folks to come and enjoy an active retirement in an "age separate" community. That concept was developing at the same time American society's view of retirement was shifting. Before World War II, most retirees stayed in their own neighborhoods, but improvements in transportation and communication gave retirees the option to live wherever their hearts chose and still stay in touch. Sun City residents came from every state in the Union and from 54 foreign countries.

Since then, many other communities have sprung up based on Webb's successful retirement concept.

Snowbirds

For the same reasons people move to Arizona, large numbers of extended vacationers arrive each fall. Natives and residents affectionately refer to the thousands of winter visitors who "flock" to the state when snow begins to fly in the Midwest, Northeast and Canada, as snowbirds. Many winter visitors come to take a "look-see" with the possiblity of permanent relocation in their minds.

The Arizona State University Center for Business Research studies this annual phenomenon. They define a snowbird as someone who stays for one month or longer.

The typical snowbird is 60-75 years old with an average household income of $32,000. Most are from the northern tier states (west of Illinois). The largest numbers are from Minnesota, Iowa, Illinois, North Dakota, Washington and Oregon. Twenty percent of Arizona's snowbirds are from Canada. A high percentage are from rural areas and small towns. Most arrive before January and stay until March or April.

The most popular roosting place for snowbirds is in the metro Phoenix East Valley. Parks in the Phoenix area (including Apache Junction in the East Valley) contain more than 56,000 mobile home spaces and nearly 45,000 RV/travel trailer spaces. Snowbirds contribute to the state's rental, sales, fuel and utility taxes.

The researchers estimated that 300,000 snowbirds migrate to Arizona each year spending $600 million while they are in the state.

The Phoenix metropolitan area isn't the only winter destination. Tucson entertains 30,000 to 35,000 snowbirds each year. Yuma's population doubles between October and April. Casa Grande and Quartzsite are also popular winter spots.

Diversity

Occasionally, newcomers unacquainted with Arizona arrive expecting to find a barren, Sahara-style desert. They soon discover that there aren't many sand dunes here, although there is an abundance of sand and rock. Once you've become accustomed to the change of scenery you'll discover Arizona's Sonoran desert is overflowing with life and vegetation. While unlike the lush green of the Northwest or a midwestern summer, Arizona is tinted from a palette of browns, tans, and grey greens. Native flowering plants are predominantly yellow. Brittle bush, palo verde and poppies carpet the state in the springtime. Other plants, such as the giant saguaro cacti and the Joshua trees are covered with clusters of white waxy flowers. Many of the smaller cacti boldly announce their presence in flaming reds and magentas.

The state has three distinctive topographic regions:
- High plateau area
- Mountainous area
- Desert valley and low mountainous area

Arizona has natural geographic divisions that occur on a diagonal from northwest to southeast. The desert valleys and the low mountains are in the south. Long stretches of plateau are broken by mountains and canyons in the northern high country. The highest point is Humphrey's Peak near Flagstaff at 12,663 feet, and the lowest (only 70 feet above sea level) is near Yuma.

The Colorado River and its tributaries have cut beautiful canyons into the otherwise flat land of northern Arizona. In addition to the Grand Canyon, other breathtaking canyons include Oak Creek Canyon, Canyon de Chelly (Canyon d' Shay), and Walnut Canyon.

Geographic Regions

The Mogollon (Muggy-OWN) Rim marks the southern boundary of the plateau areas. An awesome geological fault, the Rim is a steep rock wall nearly 2,000 feet high, extending east/west from central Arizona to southwestern New Mexico. Its multi-colored rock is sprinkled with pine, manzanita, and shrub oak. Southern Arizonans often head for the Rim in mid-

Arizona's Major Peaks

Mount Humphreys	12,670 feet
Mount Agassiz	12,340 feet
Mount Fremont	11,940 feet
Mount Baldy	11,550 feet
Escudillo Mountain	10,955 feet
Mount Ord	10,860 feet
Mount Graham	10,717 feet
Kendrick Mountain	10,418 feet
Mount Wrightson	9,458 feet
Bill Williams Mountain	9,256 feet
Mount Lemmon	9,157 feet

summer to refresh their spirits in the midst of the world's largest stand of Ponderosa pine.

Nearly a quarter of the state (30,000 square miles) is covered by mountains. The San Francisco Peaks near Flagstaff and the White Mountains in eastern Arizona are the most prominent. Other significant ranges include the Hualapai (WAHL-uh-pie) Mountains south of Kingman, the Bradshaws near Sedona, the Superstitions east of Phoenix, and the Catalinas just outside of Tucson. Many of the mountains are covered with trees, but dry desert mountains with creosote bushes, palo verde trees, and cacti are also common.

Arizona is one of the few states which has all six life zones. The Lower Sonoran Zone, with elevations under 4,500 feet, is hot and dry with arid plains, barren mountains, and saguaro cacti. Animals in that zone often retreat to a den or burrow during the heat of the day. In contrast, the Alpine Zone found in the San Francisco Peaks can bring freezing temperatures even in mid-summer. Dwarf plants and trees characterize this zone.

The state's rare geological formations make it a paradise for rock hounds. Rocks of all sizes, shapes and derivations are abundant. The most common mineral is copper. Gold, petroleum, pumice, silver, uranium, and zinc are also found. Gemstones, including turquoise, fire agate, peridot, amethyst, and opal, are also in good supply here.

Water

Even in this desert state, there are rivers and lakes. Arizona's great water lifeline is the Colorado River. It runs through 688 miles of the state, flowing down from Utah, winding through the Grand Canyon, then turning south to divide Arizona and California. At the end of 1985, the Central Arizona Project (CAP), began delivering water from the Colorado River to Phoenix. The 190-mile stretch had been under development since 1968. CAP reached Tucson in 1991 when the remaining 143-mile waterline was completed. CAP delivers 1.5 million acre-feet to Arizona's interior each year for the cities, farms and Indian reservations. (Just how much is an acre foot of water? 325,851 gallons.) Water is also available from the Salt River Project, wells and ground water.

Although Arizona rivers may appear dry, water is almost always flowing beneath the surface. Bridges over dry river beds look strange to new Arizonans, but in a thunderstorm waterless rivers can quickly become raging torrents.

The Salt River runs through Phoenix. Most of the time the water is held behind dams in the canyons or is channeled through the city by the Salt River Project canals. The Salt meets the Verde River east of Phoenix and flows into the Gila River at Gila Bend in western Arizona. Tucson has three major rivers or washes—the Santa Cruz River, Rillito River, and Pantano Wash.

The Salt River Canyon north of Globe on US 60 is spectacular, bearing a striking resemblance to the Grand Canyon with vertical rock walls, multicolored spires and buttes. The drive winds down into the canyon, dropping more than 2,000 feet in five miles of plummeting switchbacks.

Many mountain creeks flow all year. Small natural lakes can be found in the high country. All the state's larger lakes, including Roosevelt and San Carlos lakes, Lake Mead, Lake Havasu, and Lake Powell are man-made. Lakes Powell and Mead have the distinction of being the two largest artificial lakes in America and Roosevelt Dam is the world's largest masonry dam.

Land

Stretching 400 miles from top to bottom and 310 miles across, Arizona is the nation's sixth largest state, covering 113,417 square miles (72.7 million acres), with 492 square miles of water within the borders.

Just how large is the state? All six New England states plus Pennsylvania and Delaware would fit nicely within its borders. Twice the size of New York, Arizona has 33 people per square mile. That is a twelfth of New York's 370.8 per square mile. It is little wonder that Arizona has become known as a state of wide open spaces. With the tenth lowest population density in the United States, even the urban centers have plenty of elbow room. The city of Phoenix, with 251,648 acres (393.2 square miles) still averages a quarter of an acre per individual.

Not all of Arizona's land is available for development, however. Actually only a small portion, 18 percent, is owned by individuals or corporations.

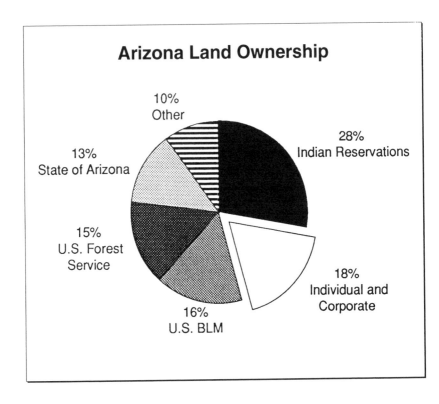

Climate

Ask any newcomer why he came to Arizona and somewhere near the top of the list will be "the weather." Wherever you are in Arizona, it's only a short drive to a change of scene. Variations in altitude and terrain account for some of the most diverse weather patterns in the nation, but sunshine is the common denominator. Yearly average precipitation ranges from two and a half inches in the southwest corner of the state to 27 inches in the White Mountains. Most of the state's precipitation occurs during the monsoon season in July and August.

Precipitation for U.S. Cities (In Inches)

City	Snowfall	Rain
Phoenix	trace	7.1
Boston	42.6	42.5
Chicago	43.0	34.4
Detroit	31.7	30.9
Miami	None	59.8
Minneapolis	46.5	25.9
New York	29.2	40.1
St. Louis	19.5	35.8
Seattle	7.9	38.6

Source: National Weather Service

Even in the cold regions, the sun still shines brightly day after day. On occasion, both the nation's high and low temperature readings are registered in Arizona on the same day.

Summer in southern Arizona is hot and dry, but winters are warm and pleasant. Air conditioning permits residents to live in year-round comfort. The highest official temperature ever recorded in Arizona was 127 degrees in 1896 at Fort Mohave and in 1905 at Parker. The hottest temperature ever recorded in Phoenix was 122.

Northern Arizona has four distinctive seasons. Residents there expect 15 to 70 inches of snowfall each year. Summers are cool and pleasant. Winter in the high country is cool with temperatures often hovering around 15 degrees.

Average Yearly Precipitation for Arizona Cities

City	Snowfall (Inches)	Rain (Inches)
Phoenix	Trace	7.10
Tucson	.6	10.73
Flagstaff	84.4	19.80
Yuma	None	2.99
Prescott	23.7	18.10
Sedona	8.8	17.15
Lake Havasu City	None	3.82
Casa Grande	None	8.12

Source: National Weather Service

Since the sun shines four out of five days, its presence or absence accounts for dramatic differences in temperature. In the summer, when daytime temperatures exceed the century mark, residents wait for sunset to pursue outdoor activities. Even trips to the grocery store are frequently delayed until the sun begins to sink and asphalt parking lots cool. In winter, sunset brings a rapid drop in temperature.

Some months it's not at all unusual to drive with the air conditioning on in the daytime and switch to the heater that evening. Even if you live in the state's warmer zones, after a short time in Arizona you'll be digging out some of those warm winter sweaters, lightweight jackets, and occasionally even a heavy coat to warm up when temperatures in Phoenix and Tucson dip below freezing.

In summer, when the eastern portions of the United States are sweltering under sultry conditions day and night, Arizona is often more tolerable, even at higher temperatures. At higher

Apparent Temperature

Humidity (%)	Air Temperature (In degrees)							
	80	85	90	95	100	105	110	115
0%	73	78	83	87	91	95	99	103
10%	75	80	85	90	95	100	105	111
20%	77	82	87	93	99	105	112	120
30%	78	84	90	96	104	113	123	135
40%	79	86	93	101	110	123	137	151
50%	81	88	96	107	120	135	150	
60%	82	90	100	114	132	149		
70%	85	93	106	124	144			
80%	86	97	113	136				
90%	88	102	122					
100%	91	108						

elevations, summer days are mild with crisp evenings.

You'll often hear, "But it's a dry heat." The low humidity helps your body cool more efficiently by allowing perspiration to evaporate quickly. That's why you'll feel as comfortable as if the temperature were lower and the humidity higher. The "apparent temperature" chart shows the effect of humidity on how warm it will actually seem.

During the winter months the effects of low relative humidity are less noticeable, although you may need additional moisturizing lotion for your skin and a conditioner for your hair. Colds seem to go away faster and feel less severe because of the low humidity.

You'll often hear Arizona weather forecasters refer to the *dew point*, the temperature at which water can condense in the atmosphere. The dew point varies with the temperature, but not as much as relative humidity. If the dew point is below 55 degrees, evaporative coolers operate efficiently.

Lifestyle

Whether you're in a rural village or an urban center, you'll find the emphasis on relaxation. Since Arizona is one of the nation's playgrounds, people have flocked to the state to kick back and enjoy themselves. Residents have taken their cue and adopted a philosophy of taking time to stop and enjoy the beauty that surrounds them. With the state's accommodating climate for outdoor activities, Arizonans step out of their front doors into one gigantic recreation room.

There's swimming, tennis, golf, hiking, boating, skiing, fishing, rock hounding and many other activities. A pleasant side effect of all those activities is a slimmer, trimmer, healthier citizenry. The active lifestyle that most Arizona seniors lead contributes to an improved quality of life. You'll find universal agreement that it beats sitting around watching it snow.

Visitors are often struck by the practical approach Arizonans take to life and the innovative ways they deal with the warm summer temperatures. Even the finer restaurants take a relaxed approach to dress. It's unlikely you'll be asked to find a tie or put on a jacket. Restaurants have been known to cut off the ties of their patrons and mount them alongside thousands that have been worn into the restaurant, but not worn out.

In the summer, outdoor workers get an early start so they can finish work before the heat of the day. Whether they're off for a siesta or a cool drink in the shade, the day ends early.

Most offices have flexible dress codes that put workers' comfort before formality. You'll find most suit coats make their way to the back of the closet from April to September.

Health

Many residents came to Arizona in pursuit of better health. You'll find conflicting opinions, however, about whether the climate will actually improve your health. Once considered a haven for allergy sufferers, many people who arrive with sniffles and sneezes find temporary relief before becoming vulnerable to a new set of local pollens. Unfortunately, some non-indigenous trees and plants have become year-round pollen-bearers. The most notorious of these plants are Bermuda grass, olive and mulberry trees. Some cities even have bans on certain plants.

If you're considering a move to Arizona for health reasons, you should check with your doctor to see whether a move to a hot to cool, dry climate would be beneficial to your condition. Still, while a few ailments may be aggravated by the climate here, stories of miracle cures abound. There's more than one resident who arrived in poor health and made a remarkable recovery. Whether that can be attributed to the humidity, the heat, the sunshine, or just a change in attitude, no one can be sure.

Economy

Arizona's economy largely depends on manufacturing, tourism, and services. Mining and agriculture are also significant, although they have dwindled in importance. Arizona is a leading producer of cattle, cotton and citrus. Yields from Arizona's irrigated cropland are among the highest in the nation. Fifteen hundred years ago the Hohokam Indians took advantage of the level land along the Salt River to develop an extensive system of irrigation canals for their farms. Cattlemen and cowboys began settling in Arizona in the 1870s and 1880s. These ranchers were attracted by the abundance of grasses and the mild climate. By the turn of the century cotton and citrus farms could be found in the central part of the state.

Today, Arizona farms also produce vegetables, hay, fruit crops, and milk as well as a multitude of specialty crops, including jojoba, napa, bok choy, and guayle. To the shopper that means locally grown lettuce, onions, broccoli, cauliflower and honeydew melons arrive fresh at the supermarket.

Arizona produces 65 percent of all copper mined in the United States, although an abundant worldwide copper supply has caused many Arizona copper mines to shut down. Together, agriculture and mining now contribute only 2 percent of Arizonans' personal income.

More than 350,000 workers in Arizona are employed in wholesale or retail trades accounting for more than 50 percent of the state's jobs. Services account for nearly as many jobs. Manufacturing employed nearly 176,500 people during 1991, half in the state's 700 hightech companies. Construction employs about 6 percent of the workforce.

Sixteen million visitors come to Arizona each year. Tourism brings $5 billion into the state and keeps 70,000 people busy, while another 114,000 provide support services and products for tourism and related businesses. The Phoenix and Valley of the Sun Convention and Visitor's Bureau estimates that overall nine million visitors come to the metropolitan Phoenix area each year spending $2.9 billion annually.

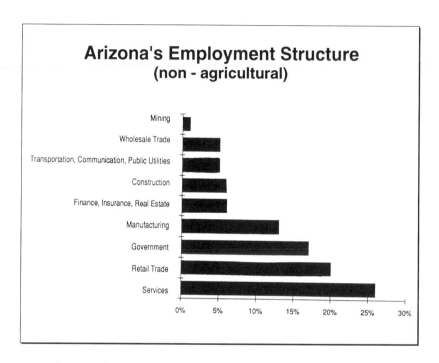

Arizona's Employment Structure
(non - agricultural)

Job growth was particularly strong in Arizona during the mid-1980s. A slowdown occurred late in the decade, but signs of recovery were abundant by 1993, with housing starts, in-state migration and money supplies all showing positive signs.

Arizona's unemployment rate has traditionally been lower than the national average. That's due in part to the broad base of economic activity which insulates Arizona from bad times in any particular industry. Even when times are bad in Arizona, they aren't much worse than normal in most other parts of the country.

Growth

Arizona's dynamic growth could keep a staff of statisticians busy crunching numbers trying to keep track of what's happening to people, jobs and industry. Migration to the Sun

Belt began after World War II and picked up dramatically during the 1970s. Why? Climate, lack of congestion, and established retirement communities all contributed.

In the decade between 1970 and 1980, the U.S. population grew by 11 percent, while Arizona grew by 53 percent. The influx of newcomers peaked in 1985, and during 1988 and 1989 the growth spurt slowed a bit. Another surge is expected in the early 1990s.

When Arizona became a state in 1912, only 200,000 people lived here. The Arizona Department of Economic Security estimates by the turn of the century the number will be 4.8 million. Currently, more than three and a half million people reside in Arizona. Maricopa County is expected to be home to three million and Pima County will shelter nearly 900,000 by the year 2000.

2

Getting Acquainted

Coming of Age

Arizona was already inhabited 15,000 years ago and prehistoric creatures roamed the area millions of years ago. In 1984, 225 million year-old dinosaur bones, the oldest ever found, were uncovered in northern Arizona's Petrified Forest.

Three early Indian tribes settled the area, the Anasazi (An-a-SAH-ze) in the north, the Hohokam (Ho-HO-kam) in the Salt and Gila (Hee-LAH) River valleys and the Mogollon in the east. Between the time of Christ and 1300 A.D., the Anasazi occupied the Four Corners region where Arizona, New Mexico, Utah, and Colorado meet. They are believed to be the ancestors of the modern day Hopi Indians. The Anasazi left behind extensive artifacts including pottery, turquoise, jewelry, woven baskets, cotton clothing, stone tools, and mummies. In recent years, their relics have become valuable collectors' items and have made their way into the black market. A crackdown on pothunting, however, has slowed looting of the Anasazi sites. The 1979 Archaeological Resources Protection Act makes pothunting on federal land a felony punishable by up to a $250,000 fine and two years in jail. The Anasazi left another reminder of their civilization that all Arizona residents and visitors can enjoy. Throughout the Southwest, ancient Anasazi petroglyphs (carved images) and pictographs (painted images) can be found on canyon walls.

By 200 A.D. an agricultural tribe of Indians known as the Hohokam moved into Arizona, staying for about a thousand years. The Hohokam built a complex system of irrigation canals, however, these early inhabitants seemed to have disappeared from the region about the time Columbus was setting sail for the New World.

In the sixteenth century, Spaniards, including Coronado, came north from Mexico in search of the gold-plated Seven Cities of Cibola. The region was sparsely populated with Indian settlements until the 17th century. The name Arizona probably came from "*ali shonak,*" small place of the spring," in the Tohono O'odham (Papago) Indian language.

Shortly before European settlers came, the Apache and Navajo tribes moved into the area. Late in the seventeenth century Father Eusibio Kino, a Jesuit priest, began establishing missions in Arizona. Among the most famous and probably most photographed is the "White Dove of the Desert," the Mission San Xavier del Bac near Tucson.

In 1752, the first white settlement was established at Tubac by Spanish troops. A few years later in 1776, a Spanish fort and missionary outpost were set up at Tucson. In the following 80 years, the Arizona territory passed from Spain to Mexico to the United States. By the late 1860s, Tucson was a thriving metropolis of 3,000. Now, 130 years later, it has grown to well over 400,000 residents.

Geronimo and Apache Warriors

Congress created the Arizona Territory on December 17, 1863, at about the same time white men were resettling the old Hohokam campgrounds, where the city of Phoenix now stands. By then, Tucson was already a vital southern supply depot and the territorial capital.

Early white settlers fought bitterly with raiding Indians bands. Among well-known Apache chiefs of that era were Cochise, Geronimo, and Mangas Colorados. Under Geronimo's leadership, the Apaches finally surrendered on September 4, 1886, two years after the Navajo surrendered to Kit Carson.

Descendants of the early Spanish, Mexican, and Indian settlers still live in Arizona. Their cultural contribution can be seen in the architecture, food, clothing, decorating, art, language, and lifestyle of the Southwest.

Miners came with the discovery of gold and silver. Copper mines flourished in the 1870s and 1880s. A number of

Arizona's sedate rural communities once had rowdy pasts associated with the early mining days. In the late 1860s, farmers in the Salt River Valley began irrigating their fields and in the next ten years ranching became big business. On February 14, 1912, Arizona became the 48th state, the last of the contiguous states.

Indian Reservations

Arizona is home to 14 Indian tribes and many of their members (165,000) make their homes on the 19,555,000 acres of reservation land within Arizona's borders. The reservations range in size from the 85-acre Tonto-Apache Reservation near Payson to the 14,775,068-acre Navajo nation which crosses Arizona's borders into Utah and New Mexico.

Each of the state's twenty reservations is a sovereign nation within the boundaries of the United States, with its own tribal government, laws, culture, and customs. Visitors to the reservations are under the jurisdiction of tribal, not Arizona state law. The reservations are administered by the Bureau of Indian Affairs. In recent years, the tribal councils have taken a more active role in governing the reservations, dealing with local, state, and federal governments, and negotiating with private industry.

In 1924, the Indian Citizenship Act gave citizenship rights to every Indian born within the territorial United States. Indians living on reservations pay all federal and state taxes, but do not pay taxes on reservation lands and property. Indians who do not live on reservations pay the same taxes as other citizens. All Indians have full voting rights.

Arizona Indians are internationally known for their woven tapestries, basketry, jewelry, pottery, Kachina dolls, sand paintings, and other artwork.

For more specific information about Arizona's Indian tribes, contact:

The Arizona Commission on Indian Affairs
1645 W. Jefferson St.
Phoenix, AZ 85007
(602) 542-3123

Government

Executive

The remainder of the state is governed by three branches of state government. The Executive Department includes the governor, secretary of state, attorney general, state treasurer, and the superintendent of public instruction. Other elected state officials include a three-member Corporation Commission, and a mine inspector.

Legislative

The State Legislature includes one senator and two representatives from each of 30 legislative districts, totalling 30 Senators and 60 Representatives. Districts range from small, densely populated areas in downtown Phoenix to large sprawling districts in the rural areas that have more canyons, mesas and rock formations than people.

Bills can become law either by passing through committees, floor debates, and chamber votes or they can be ushered through by lawmakers whose influence and position enable them to control the fate of legislation. In the House, bills are assigned to three committees. The House speaker makes committee assignments, giving the speaker much control over the fate of a bill.

The Legislature meets about four months of the year. January, February, April, and May are the heaviest working months. Floor debates are usually held on Thursdays.

You can learn the current status of a bill by calling the House of Representatives Information Desk at 542-4221 or the Senate Information Desk at 542-3559.

Judicial

The State Supreme Court has five justices, each of whom serves a six-year term. The chief justice is elected for a five-year term by the justices, as is the vice chief justice.

The Arizona Court of Appeals has two geographic divisions. Sessions are usually held in Tucson or Phoenix. Cases are heard by three-member panels, and require a majority to render a decision.

Members of the State Supreme Court and the Court of Appeals are appointed by the governor.

Elections

State primary and general elections are held in even-numbered years. The governor, secretary of state, attorney general, state treasurer, and superintendent of public instruction serve four-year terms. State senators, representatives and the state mine inspector serve two-year terms. Primaries are held in September preceding the November general election. To vote in the state primary you must indicate a party preference when you register.

Party Politics

Precinct committeemen are elected to two-year terms during the primary elections. There are nearly 2,000 precincts in the state. Arizona does not have a presidential primary.

There are more than 873,000 registered Republicans in the state. The Republican Party has a statewide convention each year. Precinct committeemen select state and county chairmen in alternating years.

Republican State Headquarters
3501 N. 24th St.
Phoenix, AZ 85016
957-7770

Registered Democrats include more than 828,000 voters. Each January elected state committeemen meet to choose the party's executive committee. County chairmen are elected for two-year terms at a countywide meeting held in late fall.

Democratic State Headquarters
1509 N. Central Ave
Phoenix, AZ 85004
257-9136

Among other registered voters are 5,200 Libertarians and 232,000 non-partisan or other party affiliations.

Libertarian State Headquarters
P.O. Box 501
Phoenix, AZ 85001
248-8425

Initiative/Referendum/Recall

Statewide propositions appear on the general-election ballot. In Arizona, public office holders may face a recall election if enough registered voters sign petitions indicating they want a new election.

Arizona's State Capitol, Phoenix

County Government

Arizona's 15 counties are governed by three-member boards of supervisors, elected every two years.

The county supervisors, attorney, sheriff, treasurer, assessor, recorder, school superintendent, and clerk of the Superior Court are elected to four-year terms in even-numbered years.

Superior Court judges in Maricopa and Pima counties are appointed to four-year terms by the governor. They may then run for retention on the general election ballot. Superior Court judges in other counties run in the primary and are elected in the general election to four-year terms. Justices of the peace and constables are elected to four year terms.

You'll frequently find charts and references to particular counties. It's a good way to provide information about specific geographic areas. For more information on Arizona's 15 counties consult Appendix B.

Taxes

One reason Arizona has grown so rapidly is the state's "hands off" approach to taxation. Taxation and government in general are kept to a minimum. A study conducted by the Advisory Commission on Intergovernmental Relations found that Arizona residents paid a typical income tax bill of $225, sales tax of $554 per year and property tax of $468, ranking Arizona 24th when compared with other states.

A number of tax law changes were under consideration by the legislature as of this writing. For more current information, contact:

Arizona Department of Revenue
Taxpayer Assistance
P.O. Box 29086
Phoenix, AZ 85038
From Phoenix: 255-3381
From Tucson: 628-6421
From other Arizona locations: (800) 352-4090

Expect a written reply to take from 4-6 weeks.

Property Taxes

Property taxes vary widely, depending upon which taxing bodies have jurisdiction over a parcel. Cities, school districts, fire districts, and costs associated with electric districts and street improvements may be included on a tax bill.

An assessed valuation is determined, then property tax is calculated based on a specified percentage of the assessed valuation. Rates vary by category:

- Owner occupied residential property, 10 percent
- Vacant and agricultural property, 16 percent
- Commercial property, 25 percent
- Rental property, 14 percent

Taxes are paid in two installments. The first half is due on November 1; the second half by May 1.

The following rules apply to property taxation in Arizona:

- Counties, cities and community colleges are limited to an increase in total property tax levels of two percent over the previous year's levels, plus or minus the net change in construction.
- The valuation of locally-valued property is limited to a 10 percent growth over the prior year's limited value.
- The maximum tax liability for residential property is one percent of full cash value.
- Owner-occupied residential properties are assessed at 10 percent of full cash value.
- The state tax rate as of 1992 was 66 cents per $100 of assessed valuation. Other property taxes are levied locally and vary from one area to another.

Property tax exemptions are available for widows, widowers, and the disabled, including veterans. Contact the county assessor's office for more information on these exemptions. If you rent housing for six months or more, you may qualify for a tax credit on your state income tax return.

Sales Tax

The state imposes sales taxes ranging from 3/8 to 5 percent on business activities. Retail items are taxed at 5 percent. In addition to the state tax rate, 67 municipalities impose a 1 or 2 percent tax on tax bases which are usually narrower than state definitions. Food and pharmaceutical sales are not taxed. A list of sales tax rates for each city can be obtained from:

Arizona Department of Revenue
P.O. Box 29002
Phoenix, AZ 85038

Individual Income Taxes

Residents and non-residents earning income in Arizona must pay personal income tax. Deductions on the state return are more generous than the federal return. Federal and state income taxes and dividends from Arizona corporations doing 50 percent or more of their business in Arizona are given special deductions. State income tax credits are allowed for elderly, low-income taxpayers, and renters (including mobile home lots). Arizona tax rates are calculated from the federal adjusted gross income figure. You may elect to make voluntary contributions to "good causes" on your tax return. Such programs as the prevention and treatment of child abuse and Arizona wildlife benefit. If your gross income will be less than $100,000 for the year, you are not required to make estimated state income tax payments. There is no payment for underpayment. You are not required to make quarterly payments or have money withheld from a pension. State and federal pensions receive a $2500 exemption from state income taxes. Social Security and railroad retirement benefits are not taxed in Arizona.

Estate Taxes

Overall, Arizona's estate and inheritance taxes are lower than any other state's. The actual amount will vary depending upon the amount of the net estate, personal property, and whether you have adult children.

A return must be filed with the Arizona Department of Revenue if the gross estate exceeds $600,000. The tax rates imposed on the remaining estate are designed to absorb the maximum credit for state death taxes allowed by the federal government.

Arizona Individual Income Tax

Single and/or Married Taxpayers Filing Separately:

Taxable Income at Least	But Less Than	Pays
$0	$10,000	3.80% of taxable income
$10,001	$ 25,000	$380, plus 4.40% of the excess over $10,000
$25,001	$50,000	$1,040, plus 5.25% of the excess over $25,000
$50,001	$105,000	$ 2,352.50, plus 6.50% of the excess over $50,000
$150,001	and over	$ 8,852.50, plus 7.0% of the excess over $150,000

Married Taxpayers Filing Joint Returns
and Unmarried Heads of Households:

Taxable Income at Least	But Less Than	Pays
$0	$20,000	3.80% of taxable income
$ 20,001	$50,000	$760, plus 4.40% of the excess over $20,000
$50,001	$100,000	$2,080, plus 5.25% of the excess over $50,000
$100,001	$ 300,000	$4,705, plus 6.50% of the excess over $100,000
$300,001	and over	$17,705, plus 7.0% of the excess over $300,000

Returns on taxable estates must be filed with the Department of Revenue Estate Tax Division within nine months after death.

Gasoline and Motor Vehicle Taxes

Gasoline and diesel fuel are taxed by the state at 18 cents per gallon. The annual vehicle registration fee is $8.00 per vehicle, while new vehicle registrations are $12. In addition, the motor vehicle tax is calculated "ad valorem" in lieu of property taxes. The initial tax base is computed at 60 percent of the manufacturer's list price, without options. The fee is reduced by 13 percent each year. The tax rate is $4 per $100 of assessed valuation with a minimum tax set at $23.33. Renewals are on a staggered system throughout the year, generally in the same month the plates were initially issued. The license plates remain with the vehicle and a sticker is applied to the license each year to indicate the tags are up-to-date. Disabled veterans are exempt from vehicle license tax and registration fees.

Community Property

As a community property state, real or personal property acquired by either husband or wife during a marriage may be considered community property of both. If you are moving from a state that does not have a community property law, check with an attorney to be sure your will complies with Arizona state law.

As a general rule, property acquired before a marriage and property acquired by one spouse by gift or inheritance is considered separate property. Virtually everything else acquired during a marriage is community property.

An important exception exists for joint tenancy property. On the death of one joint tenant, the property passes to the remaining joint tenant.

Arizona is a no-fault divorce state. Community property laws affect divorce settlements. In fixing the amount and duration of alimony, the court considers the contribution one spouse made to the earning ability of the other, as well as any income or career sacrifices a spouse may have made for the other's benefit. The court also considers the ability of both parties to contribute to the costs of educating their children. They also give weight to marriages of long duration if a spouse's age might prevent finding suitable employment after the divorce or legal separation.

Getting Married

Getting married is a simple procedure in the state if you are 22 or older. No blood test or waiting period is required. Licenses can be obtained at the local justice courts for slightly less than $25.

Lottery

Proceeds from sale of state lottery tickets are used to fund public transportation; street lighting and repair; and senior citizen vans. The state keeps approximately 30 cents of each dollar played, with the rest paid out in winnings. Grand prize winners receive their money over a period of 20 years with taxes deducted in advance. Tickets are sold at a variety of retail outlets and drawings are held on Saturday and Wednesday evenings.

If no one has picked all six winning numbers for the week the jackpot accumulates to the next drawing. Numbers can be selected individually or the computer will randomly select your numbers in a "quick pick."

There is also an instant "scratch off" game. Themes for the scratch game change frequently.

Officially Speaking

State Capitol

In 1889, Moses H. Sherman, owner of the Arizona Improvement Company, Marcellus E. Collins and their wives donated ten acres of land to the Territory of Arizona on which to build a state capitol. The site is bordered by 17th and 18th avenues and Adams and Jefferson streets in Phoenix.

The original capitol building is flanked by newer buildings, and now houses the Capitol Museum. The Ionic-Grecian structure is topped by a 45-foot copper dome and a 16-foot weather vane, the "Winged Victory." The copper for the dome was donated by the state's copper industry.

An anchor from the Battleship *U.S.S. Arizona* rests on the east end of the Capitol Mall. A bronze plaque lists all the sailors and marines who died on board during the attack on Pearl Harbor, December 7, 1941.

Statehood

On February 14, 1912, President William Howard Taft signed into law the act that made Arizona the nation's 48th state. The state is often called the **Valentine State** since admission to the Union coincided with that holiday.

State Flag

The Arizona state flag represents the setting sun with 13

alternating red and yellow rays in the upper half over a blue field. A copper-colored star shines from the center of the setting sun. Official state colors are blue and gold.

State Bird

The **cactus wren,** a woody brown bird with a speckled breast, is the official state bird. At home in thorny desert plants, the wren is frequently found nesting in arms of giant saguaro cacti.

State Flower

The blossom of the giant **saguaro cactus,** the largest cactus found in the United States, is the official Arizona flower.

Found almost exclusively in Arizona and northern Mexico, pure white, waxy flowers appear in garlands on the tips of the arms in May and June.

State Tree

The **palo verde tree,** found in the desert and desert foothill regions of Arizona, takes its name from the Spanish words for "green stick."

State Gemstone

Turquoise.

Official Neckwear

Bola tie—generally a leather string with silver clasp adorned with turquoise.

State Motto

"Diat Deus," Latin for *God Enriches*.

State Slogan

"The Grand Canyon State."

3

Finding a Place

Housing choices in Arizona abound and competition for home sales and rentals is keen, which is good news for the newcomer. If your heart and budget desire, you can find housing developments with price tags beginning at $2 million. But if your tastes are a little less ostentatious, you'll find a wide variety of affordable housing, including mobile home parks, efficiency apartments, empty nester homes, and more conventional communities. There are both brand new homes and many previously-owned homes on the market. As a general rule, resale homes sell for slightly less than their never-been lived-in counterparts.

A recent count indicated nearly 19,000 permits were issued for new homes in Maricopa County during 1992. Another 5,500 permits were issued in Pima County. The average permit value in Maricopa County was $110,250. In the Tucson area permit values averaged $100,500. Hot spots for new

Maricopa County Median Sales Prices

Ahwatukee/Foothills...................... $118,700
Avondale.. 106,950
Carefree/Cave Creek....................... 167,500
Chandler.. 90,800
Gilbert... 102,650
Glendale.. 75,000
Mesa 79,000
Paradise Valley............................... 295,325
Peoria 84,000
Phoenix... 74,500
Scottsdale 125,600
Sun City 64,800
Sun City West................................. 109,000
Tempe... 86,000

Source: Arizona Real Estate Center, L. William Seidman

Research Institute, College of Business, Arizona State University, 1993

construction were in Mesa, Gilbert, Chandler, Glendale, Peoria, Scottsdale, Phoenix and Tucson.

Because there are so many choices at so many prices, you'll do best if you first take a look at where you want to be, what type of housing will suit your needs, and how much you can afford to spend.

Some points to consider:

- Do you want warm temperatures all year long or do you prefer a four-season climate?
- Do you like the hustle and bustle of city life, or does life in a small town or slightly out-of-town appeal to you?

- How important is it to be near major medical facilities, public transportation, and airports?
- What will your lifestyle be like? Will you entertain or have frequent out-of-state visitors? Is golf or tennis in the plans?
- Do you want to live in a community where residents are about your own age? Do you prefer adults only, or a mixture of ages?
- How much can you afford to spend on housing?
- Will you be a year-round resident or spend your summers elsewhere?

Answers to these questions will help narrow your choices, but the possibilities are still overwhelming.

In Appendix A, you'll find more than 40 Arizona communities profiled. Once you know exactly what you're looking for, you can target a few locations for up-close inspection. A visit to Arizona is your best way to get acquainted. Some developments offer special get-acquainted plans.

For many retirees, a retirement community is just what they've dreamed about, but others are just as adamant about wanting to live where there are people of all ages.

Arizona allows municipalities to make public ordinances which establish age-specific community zoning districts. In some cases whole communities are affected, and in others just certain developments.

These laws require that the head of the household or spouse must be a specific age or older. In Sun City for instance, the head of household must be at least 55 years old. Minors are also prohibited from living in the home.

Age-specific community zoning districts cannot be overlaid over property without permission of *all* property owners of the property in the district unless the property has been developed,

Where the Retirees Are

County	Residents 55-64	Residents 65+	Percentage of Population 55+
Yavapai	14,103	22,148	35.5
Mohave	13,332	16,599	33.1
La Paz	1,841	3,403	34.8
Gila	4,904	7,044	27.7
Pima	59,167	90,546	21.6
Pinal	11,380	16,065	23.9
Yuma	8,969	14,036	23.1
Cochise	9,760	12,464	21.1
Maricopa	164,451	260,588	19.9
Santa Cruz	2,481	3,400	19.6
Greenlee	751	832	18.6
Navajo	5,905	6,143	14.0
Coconino	5,244	6,630	12.0
Apache	3,752	4,496	11.8
Arizona	308,201	467,441	20.8

Source: Arizona Department of Economic Security
Population Statistics Unit (Based on 1990 Population Estimates)

advertised, and sold or rented under specific-age restrictions. (Arizona Revised Statutes 9-46201A11).

Other restrictions may be applied by county and city ordinances as well as deed restrictions. Maricopa County's Senior Citizen Zoning Ordinance makes it illegal for anyone 18 years of age or less to live in "senior zones." Exemptions are available from the Board of Adjustment only under hardship conditions.

Before selecting an age-restrictive community, be sure you understand exactly what the conditions are, how exemptions are made, and what the penalties for non-compliance could be.

Only in Arizona

Probably more than any other growth area of the country, Arizona (and particularly southern Arizona) has a distinctive architectural and landscaping style. Red tile roofs, tan stucco buildings, privacy walls, arches and courtyards dot the landscape.

Most Arizona homes are built of stucco, brick, slump block, cement block, burnt adobe, or combinations of those materials. Many years ago, homes were built of adobe with walls two feet thick to provide natural insulation from the heat. Today adobe homes are rare and valuable treasures. You'll find more adobe homes in the Tucson area than in Phoenix. Older houses are generally ranch style, and newer homes, Spanish Mediterranean or pueblo style architecture. Tile roofs are common on more expensive homes and asphalt shingles on less expensive models.

There are very few basements in Arizona and most older homes have carports rather than enclosed garages. Most homes use low, one-story designs. Since heating and cooling ductwork usually runs through the ceiling rather than a basement or walls, you'll often find coolers perched on the rooftops. Evaporative cooling units, or "swamp coolers," are an Arizona invention that cool by pulling air across pads of water and circulating it through the house. They are less costly to operate than air conditioners and cool quite efficiently when the temperature is below 100 degrees. You'll find many homes equipped with both cooling systems. The climate has an impact on utility bills. The power bills in the warmer areas of the state are highest in the summer and lowest in the winter.

More than 80 percent of the heating and cooling systems of new homes are powered by an electric heat pump. Heat pumps are energy efficient, operating best when the temperature is higher than 32 degrees Fahrenheit. Heat pumps require only one mechanical system. In the winter the refrigerant circulating inside the heat pump picks up heat from outside air and pumps it into the home. In the summer, heat from inside the home is absorbed and pumped outside. Tests show that heat pumps use about one fourth of the energy of a gas furnace.

Arizona homes usually feature lots of windows and large covered patios for taking maximum advantage of backyard vistas. Many residents prefer wood and metal blinds to fabric window coverings since they are easier to keep dust-free and allow rooms to be bright, yet shaded. Shade screens which cut down on the amount of heat entering the house are often found on windows facing the sun. Mexican tile, stone, brick, or flagstone are often used as interior and exterior floor covering materials.

Patios and swimming pools also help tame the summer heat. One estimate indicates that one of every seven homes in the state has a swimming pool. You'll find an endless variety of styles including play pools, lap pools, and diving pools.

Outside you'll find both desert and green landscape designs. While it may take a bit of adjustment at first, there are certainly some big dividends in choosing native plants and rock gardens. There's no need to mow, fertilize, or weed. By choosing indigenous plants, you won't be introducing plants that are unable to adjust to the climate or that have to be watered profusely. It is possible to turn an Arizona lawn into a lush, green Minnesota-style yard, but it's really not recommended. Not only is it expensive to put in, it's also costly to water and maintain.

The Arizona Native Plant Society has descriptive information about desert plants suitable for home use. You can request a brochure by writing:

> Arizona Native Plant Society
> Urban Landscape Committee
> P.O. Box 41206 Sun Station
> Tucson, AZ 85717

In addition, many city water departments provide consumer information about plants with low water needs.

Home Ownership

When it comes to purchasing a home, you'll probably choose one of two likely paths. Realtors handle both new and resale property. Many communities have Multiple Listing Services which allow all agents belonging to the service to sell any home listed. New property is often purchased directly from the builder/developer.

Most home purchase problems can be traced to rushing into the decision, looking at too many homes at one time, or not adequately checking what the home and neighborhood have to offer. If you plan on buying a previously-owned home and are not willing to risk unexpected repair bills or other surprises, you can obtain a third-party evaluation from a professional inspection firm.

Some people prefer to build custom homes. If this avenue appeals to you, check on prospective contractors by contacting:

> Registrar of Contractors
> 800 W. Washington   400 W. Congress
> Phoenix, AZ 85007   Tucson, AZ 85701
> 542-1525   628-6345

Arizona has a fund designed to compensate victims of unlawful practices by licensed real estate agents or brokers. The Arizona Real Estate Recovery Fund is financed by real estate license fees. If you have a problem, contact the Arizona Real Estate Commissioner's Office first. Certain steps must be followed in order for a claim to be paid.

Department of Real Estate
Administrative Section
2910 N. 44th St.
Phoenix, AZ 85012
468-1414

Renting

Many newcomers choose to rent a home or apartment either on a temporary or permanent basis. Even if you plan to buy a home, there are some advantages to renting first. It can give you time to get better acquainted with the community and let you make your final decision without a deadline looming. It can also give you time to see how well you really like Arizona. The drawback is that it may mean making two moves, and many people would prefer to avoid that.

Renters are eligible for a tax credit on their Arizona Personal Income Tax return. To qualify, you must be a resident for a full year and have paid rent in the state for at least six months. Public housing does not qualify.

Late spring, summer, and early fall are the best times to apartment hunt. Because of the large number of seasonal winter visitors, the selection is smaller and the prices higher in winter. You'll find giveaway publications on stands at grocery stores, convenience stores, and some Chambers of Commerce or visitor's bureaus that list apartments for rent and homes for sale. These publications can help target areas and price ranges. There are also apartment location services that help match you to the type of housing you are searching for. Their fee is usually paid by the landlord.

Before you sign any rental agreement, be sure you understand:

- Amount of rent and when it is due.
- Amount of deposit and how much of it is refundable.
- Where you can park.
- Whether the utilities are included in the rent or must be paid for separately.
- Procedure for terminating the lease.
- Rules regarding pets and pet deposits.
- Rules about using common facilities such as pool, laundry, etc.
- Who takes care of pest control.

All renters should become acquainted with the Arizona Residential Landlord and Tenant Act. You can get your own copy from:

> Secretary of State
> Capitol West Wing
> Phoenix, AZ 85007
> 542-4086

The law spells out landlord and tenant obligations. Some of the points covered by the law are discussed here. Before taking any action, you should obtain a copy of the law and read it yourself or consult a lawyer for advice. The law covers a variety of issues.

In Arizona, the landlord must provide the name of the owner or person authorized to act on the owner's behalf to whom notices and demands are to be sent. If there is a written rental agreement, both the tenant and the landlord must have copies signed by the other party. Any written rental agreement must have all blank spaces completed.

"Notice" of problems or plans to vacate must be given to the landlord in one of several ways: hand-delivered, mailed by registered or certified mail to the place of business of the landlord through which the rental agreement was made or at any place held as the place where communication is to be sent, or delivered to the designated agent. To terminate a month-to-month rental arrangement, the landlord or tenant must give at least 30 days notice prior to the periodic rental date. In other words, if you pay your rent on the first of the month and you plan to move October 1, you must notify the landlord before September 1.

An Arizona landlord cannot ask for security and prepaid rent in excess of one and a half month's rent. If cleaning and redecorating deposits are not refundable, that must be stated in writing. When the tenant moves out, property or money held as security can be applied to accumulated rent and damages. The landlord must deliver written notice to the tenant within 14 days after the tenant moves out and returns possession of the unit to the landlord, requesting return of the deposits.

The landlord must comply with all building codes affecting health and safety, make all repairs, and do what is necessary to keep the premises in a fit and habitable condition, keep all common areas in a clean and safe condition, maintain in safe and working order all electrical, plumbing, sanitary, heating, ventilating, air conditioning and other facilities and appliances.

The landlord is also required by law to provide and maintain receptacles for removal of trash. If a landlord purchases utility services and resells that service to the tenant, the amount charged cannot exceed the actual cost. While the tenant is obligated to provide access to the unit, the landlord is required to give two days notice of intent to enter. The landlord is permitted to enter without consent in case of an emergency.

The law provides that if there is "material non-compliance" with the rental agreement by the landlord, the tenant can serve written notice of the problem. If it is not remedied within 14 days, the rental agreement will terminate 30 days after the landlord receives the notice. If there is non-compliance with matters affecting health and safety, the tenant can terminate in 20 days if repairs have not been made in 10 days. Other provisions provide the tenant with substitute housing if the landlord deliberately or negligently fails to supply essential services such as running water, hot water or heat, air conditioning or cooling where such units are installed and offered.

In matters that cost less than $150 or one half of one month's rent, the tenant can correct the condition at the landlord's expense if the landlord fails to comply within 20 days. The tenant must have the work done by a licensed contractor and present an itemized statement and waiver of lien to the landlord before deducting the amount from the rent.

Arizona landlords are generally responsive to tenant problems. A 1989 court ruling allowed tenants to sue for emotional distress if a landlord fails to provide essential services.

Arizona Rental Rights: A Guidebook for Tenants, Landlords and Mobile Home Users is a valuable resource for anyone involved with a rental property.

Mobile Homes

About 10 percent of the state's residents live in mobile homes. Arizona's warm, dry climate makes this a popular choice among retirees. Per square foot, mobile homes are generally about a third the cost of conventional housing. Many planned mobile home communities offer amenities such as golf courses, saunas, and tennis courts.

The Arizona Mobile Home Association publishes a membership directory and lists nearly 250 mobile home parks by city with descriptions of each.

You can request a directory by sending $5 to:

Arizona Mobile Housing Association, Inc.
2540 E. Thomas Rd., Suite I
Phoenix, AZ 85016
955-4440

The Arizona Association of Manufactured Home Owners, Inc., is a statewide organization representing 10,000 households. The organization is actively involved with legislative activities, rent issues, and landlord-tenant disputes. For more information, contact:

Arizona Assn. of Manufactured Home Owners
20 E. Main St. #710
Mesa, AZ 85201
844-2208

The Arizona Office of Manufactured Housing oversees state laws regarding manufactured housing. For more information, contact:

Office of Manufactured Housing
State Department of Building and Fire Safety
1540 W. Van Buren St.
Phoenix, AZ 85034
255-4072

The Mobile Home Landlord-Tenant Act spells out the rights and responsibilities of landlords and tenants in mobile home parks. For the latest information, you may obtain a copy of the current version of the law by contacting:

Secretary of State
Capitol West Wing
Phoenix, AZ 85007

4

Getting Settled

Moving

Once you've made the decision to pack up and come to the sunshine state, you can start thinking about details. Moving can be a fun and exciting time filled with adventure, or it can be one headache after another.

The key to a trauma-free move is careful planning and organization. Moving is a great excuse to clean out the closets, pass on some treasured keepsakes, and donate half the goods in your closet to charity. You may even defray moving expenses with revenue from a garage sale.

Unless you're heading to northern Arizona, you won't need to bring the snow blower, shovels, or ice scrapers. Nevertheless, insiders in the moving industry say most moving vans coming from the snowbelt still arrive with at least one snow shovel on board (just in case). If you're moving to the

Phoenix or Tucson area you'll be able to clean even the heaviest frost from your windshield with an Arizona-style snow scraper—a plastic credit card!

Before loading the moving van, check to see if you are adequately insured. The movers' rates do include some insurance, but it may be substantially less than the value of your belongings. You may find yourself between policies if you are selling one house and purchasing another. Your insurance agent can write a special policy to bridge the gap.

One other important detail to check is your health insurance. Some insurance companies do not cover residents of other states. It might be necessary to change health insurance carriers when you move. This can be a concern if you have health problems.

Moving Checklist

4 Weeks Before
- [ ] Decide what to discard.
- [ ] Contact doctors, dentists and lawyers. Get copies of important papers, medical records, prescriptions, and referrals.
- [ ] Check homeowner's policy to see whether you're covered while in transit.
- [ ] Have insurance records transferred.

3 Weeks Before
- [ ] Buy fewer groceries. Use up existing stock.
- [ ] Check on service for appliances before the move.
- [ ] Dispose of flammable items and ammunition.
- [ ] Decide how your pets will be moved. Obtain certificates from the vet indicating vaccines.

☐ Notify the post office and obtain change of address forms. Send to all magazines, pen pals, business associates, etc.

2 Weeks Before

☐ Make personal travel arrangements.

☐ If you're doing the packing, get started.

☐ Close or transfer local charge accounts.

☐ Return everything you have borrowed. Retrieve anything you have in storage, on layaway, or at a friend's house.

☐ Arrange to have utilities turned off and stop other deliveries.

☐ Make a floor plan of your new home and decide where everything will go.

1 Week Before

☐ Transfer bank accounts and check to see whether your local credit bureau can send your records to your new city.

☐ Confirm travel arrangements. Pick up tickets.

☐ Arrange for money to pay the movers. (They may require cash or a certified check.)

☐ Set aside whatever you're planning to take in the car with you. Start packing suitcases.

1 Day Before Moving

☐ Set cleaning supplies aside, to be loaded last.

☐ Clean out refrigerator.

Moving Day

☐ Be on hand to keep an eye on things.

☐   Make a final check of every room and storage area.
☐   Say good-bye to friends and neighbors.

After You Arrive

You'll adjust to your new home state much more quickly if you take the initiative to get involved in your new community. Newcomers have always been welcome in Arizona because they come with enthusiasm, fresh ideas and an appreciation for the cultures and splendor that's already here. There are groups for every imaginable interest, most of whom welcome new members. Join a church group, volunteer at the local school, library or hospital. Take a class in Arizona history or learn Spanish—it'll help when reading menus and street signs. Expose yourself to different cultures and lifestyles. Seek out native Arizonans, rural Arizonans and people of various ages to provide differing points of view.

Take up a new hobby—rock hounding, birdwatching, photography and hiking are particularly inviting in Arizona. Read the newspapers to learn what's happening on the local political scene. Arizona political figures are colorful, and, even in recent years, have managed to keep most of the state sitting on the edge of their chairs expecting the unexpected.

Make a commitment to really become an Arizonan at heart. You'll be appreciated even more if you work to keep Arizona a wonderful place to live.

Voter Registration

Registering to vote in Arizona is easy. You can mail in registration forms, which can be obtained at:
  • County department of elections.
  • City clerk, county recorder's offices.

- Any party headquarters.
- Any justice of the peace.
- Any deputy registrar in your precinct.
- Driver's license examining stations.

If you are sick or disabled, a Deputy Registrar will come to your home so you may register. To vote in an Arizona election, you must:

- Be a citizen of the United States.
- Be at least 18 years old on election day.
- Have resided in the state 50 days prior to the election.
- Be able to write your own name or make your own mark (unless physically disabled).
- Never have been convicted of treason or a felony unless civil rights have been restored.
- Not be insane or under guardianship.

You must specify your political party affiliation at the time you register in order to vote in primary elections. You may also register as an independent. For some city elections, only 30-day advance registration is required.

Absentee Voting

Registered voters may vote by absentee ballot in primary and general elections if they:

- Are absent from their precinct.
- Live more than 15 miles from the polls.
- Are age 65 or older.
- Have vision defects.
- Are unable to go to the polls for physical or religious reasons.

Absentee ballots can be obtained by mail or in person from the county elections department.

Driver's Licenses

Who Needs an Arizona Driver's License?

All residents of the state must have an Arizona driver's license in order to operate a vehicle on the streets or highways of Arizona. *There is no grace period.* Arizona law requires that you obtain an Arizona license if you fit these criteria:

- Anyone, except for out-of-state students or tourists, who owns, leases, or rents a dwelling in the state and lives in it, or any person who remains in the state continuously for seven months during a calendar year.
- Anyone who engages in a trade, profession or occupation in the state or accepts employment other than seasonal agricultural work.
- Anyone who places children in a public school without paying non-resident tuition.
- Anyone who declares himself to be a resident of Arizona in order to obtain resident rates at any public educational institution.
- Any individual or business which maintains main office, branch office or warehouse facilities in the state, or operates motor vehicles in the state, or operates motor vehicles in intra-state transportation for other than seasonal agricultural work.

New Residents

Out-of-state applicants who do not have a valid driver's license in their possession must prove they have a clear driving record from the last state in which they held a license. If your license is revoked or suspended in another state, you must first meet the conditions of the previous state before you can obtain an Arizona license. The Driver's License Compact Law requires that you surrender your out-of-state license upon application for an Arizona license.

Applying for a License

Fees for licenses and registration may be paid in cash, by personal check, traveler's check or with a money order. No refunds are made on any fees. If you do not pass the required tests, you have six months or three attempts (whichever comes first) to pass. When applying, you must furnish your:
- Full name.
- Date of birth.
- Sex.
- Address.
- Previous licensing information.
- Name of the state in which the principal vehicle used is registered.

You must provide two original or certified copies of documents indicating your name, one of which must also state your date of birth. A driver's license from another state, birth or baptismal certificate, passport or alien registration certificate can be used. You'll be required to take a written test, a vision test, and have your photo taken. New drivers must also pass a road test. An Arizona Driver's License Manual will give you all the information you need to pass the written test. Manuals are available at examination stations.

Non-Driver Identification Cards

Non-drivers may apply for a permanent identification card at a Driver's License Examining Station. There is a charge for this card. These can come in handy when cashing checks or applying for services.

Licenses are valid for a lifetime up to the age of 60. Fees vary by age at the time the license is issued. Drivers must come in every 12 years for an updated photo and a vision test. Drivers over the age of 55 are issued a five-year license for $10.

Medical Conditions

A space is provided on each driver's license to note medical conditions. A signed statement from a licensed physician is needed in order to place a notation on the license.

Organ Donors

You may indicate on your driver's license if you wish to participate in the Anatomical Gift Act. A "yes" in this space permits donation of organs and tissues. This permission can be revoked at any time by signing the space indicated on the back of the license.

Name and Address Changes

You are required by law to notify the Motor Vehicle Department within 10 days if you change your name or address. If you want an updated license, you must pay an additional fee. Send the information or call:

Motor Vehicle Division
P.O. Box 2100
Mail Drop 538-M
Phoenix, AZ 85001
258-1634

Speed Limits

Arizona speed limits to remember are:

- 15 miles per hour approaching a school crossing.
- 25 miles per hour in a business or residential district.
- 55 miles per hour in most other locations.
- 65 miles per hour on most rural interstates.

Driving Under the Influence

In 1987, the Arizona legislature amended the state's DUI laws, making them among the toughest in the country. Arizona is an "implied consent" state. Anyone operating a motor vehicle in Arizona consents to a test to determine the alcohol or drug content of his blood. If you refuse to take a breath, blood or urine test, your license will be taken on the spot. The penalty is one year suspension of driving privileges. Even if the DUI charges are dismissed, your license may still be suspended for refusing to take the test. A blood alcohol content of .10 percent is evidence that you are driving while under the influence of alcohol, prescription or illegal drugs.

Penalties for driving under the influence are:

- First Offense: 24 hours in jail, $250 minimum fine, 90-day license suspension
- Second Offense within 60 months: 60 days in jail, $500 minimum fine, 1-year license revocation
- Third Offense: 6 months in jail, 3-year license revocation

The courts may also require community service or participation in treatment programs.

Vehicle Registration

Arizona law very clearly requires that new residents register their vehicles. There is a stiff fine ($300) if you fail to do so. A non-resident must register a motor vehicle in Arizona upon establishing residency, accepting employment, enrolling children in a public school or staying in the state for seven months or more during the year.

Application for registration and title is made with the County Assessor. Residents of Maricopa and Pima counties must obtain an Arizona Vehicular Inspection Certificate of Compliance from an emissions testing station before applying for registration.

For other information about vehicle or driver's licensing, contact the Motor Vehicle Division of the Arizona Department of Transportation at 255-0072.

The County Auto License Plate Department handles vehicle registrations, new license plates and title transfers in each county. For general information, call:

247-4200 in Maricopa County
624-7010 in Pima County

You will be required to:

- Turn in your out-of state plates.
- Furnish your previous registration card.
- Obtain an inspection slip, completed after physical inspection of the vehicle to verify body, style, and serial numbers by the Arizona Highway Patrol, County Assessor, or other Motor Vehicle Division agent.
- Present the previous title, if from a title state.
- Or show a manufacturer's certificate of origin with an invoice showing taxes paid, if from a non-title state, an official verification that no lien exists against the vehicle.

All owners must sign the title application and certify that the vehicle has met minimum insurance requirements.

Personalized plates are available for a one-time fee of $25, in addition to the regular costs of plates and registration.

Handicapped License Plates

A licensed Arizona physician must state in writing that the applicant meets two of the following six criteria:
- Is physically unable to make use of the public bus or train.
- Is physically unable to perform sustained work activity for more than six hours.
- Has pronounced disfigurement or deformity.
- Is physically unable to climb one flight of stairs or walk 50 yards on the level without pause.
- Has a significant loss of manual dexterity or coordination which severely restricts the performance of major life activities.

Forms for obtaining handicapped auto license plates are available from the county license plate departments. Permits are available from the State Motor Vehicle Division for temporary disabilities. Any able-bodied person parking in handicapped spaces is guilty of a misdemeanor and can be fined.

Mandatory Insurance

Arizona law requires that your vehicle be insured and the name of the insurance company and policy number be entered on an affidavit. All vehicle owners must carry $40,000 liability insurance ($15,000 injury to one person, $30,000 injury to two or more persons, and $10,000 property damage). The insurance must be purchased from a company authorized to do business in Arizona.

The vehicle owner must maintain evidence of financial responsibility in the vehicle at all times. You can meet this requirement by having one of the following in your car:

- A standard liability policy.
- A photocopy of a liability policy.
- A Certificate of Insurance.
- A copy of a $40,000 Surety Bond.
- A copy of a $40,000 Certificate of Deposit filed with the State Treasurer.
- A vehicle identification card issued by an insurance company.

If you fail to insure the vehicle, you can be fined from $250 to $750, have your driver's license and vehicle registration suspended from 90 days to three years and, in some cases, receive a jail sentence.

You must notify the Motor Vehicle Division within 10 days if you change your policy number, insurance company, or the vehicle covered on your liability insurance policy. If you do not report these changes your vehicle registration and plates can be suspended.

Emissions Testing

All vehicles manufactured after 1966, including diesels, must be emissions inspected before registration if you live in Maricopa or Pima County. You must also have an emissions test if you live outside of these two counties and commute for school or work to Maricopa or Pima County.

All gas-powered vehicles of model year 1975 or newer are checked to make sure that factory-installed emissions devices have not been removed, defeated, or altered. Some vehicles are not required to have emissions tests. They include electric-powered vehicles, golf carts, new vehicles at the time of the first sale and vehicles with engines of less than 90 cc. When you pass the emissions inspection, you will receive a Certificate of Compliance which you take to your county auto license plate department. The best time to go for testing is during the second or third week of the month. Mondays, Wednesdays and Friday evenings are also good times to go. That's when testing stations report the lines are shortest. You can call the station where you plan to be tested before you go. A recording will give an estimated wait time. Inspection fees are paid at the test station. Passenger vehicles pay $5.75.

For more specific information, call (800) 470-4646.

Firearms

Pistols or rifles may be carried openly in Arizona. Only pocket knives may be carried concealed. Sawed-off shotguns and automatic weapons are prohibited. A gun may be kept in the vehicle's glove box, but may not be hidden in a purse.

Liquor

You must be 21 years or older to purchase, serve or consume alcoholic beverages in Arizona. Alcohol may not be consumed in a vehicle or in an original container in public areas. Liquor is not sold between 1 a.m. and 7 a.m. Monday through Saturday and between 1 a.m. and 10 a.m. on Sunday.

City Driving

In Phoenix, zero point is the intersection of Central Avenue and Washington Street. Numbered streets are east of Central Avenue and run north and south. Numbered avenues are west of Central and run north and south. In Tucson, zero point is the intersection of Broadway and Stone.

Both cities have "reverse lanes" on some streets to help the rush hour traffic flow. In the mornings the center lane on these designated streets carries traffic into the city; in the evening rush hour, traffic flows out of the city in the same lane. At other, non-rush times and on weekends, the lane is used for left turns.

For your own safety, unless you are an experienced rush-hour driver, avoid venturing out on the main thoroughfares during rush hour, until you have had some experience with Arizona traffic. When thousands of commuters are rushing to work, traffic can become intimidating, especially if you're not yet familiar with where you need to turn or change lanes. Even the freeways are quite manageable between 9 a.m. and 2 p.m. and again after 6:00 p.m. on weekdays.

Pets

All dogs older than four months coming into the state must be vaccinated and licensed within 30 days of entry. Cats do not have to be vaccinated or licensed. To obtain a dog license, you must have a valid rabies vaccination certificate for your animal. If your pet has recently been vaccinated in another state, obtain a certificate from your vet before you move.

In Arizona you can be charged with a felony if you knowingly allow a vicious dog that attacks or endangers people to run at large. You must post a warning if there is a vicious animal on your property. Most cities and towns have laws requiring all dogs be on a leash, even when they are on the owner's private property. In some cases, the county also has leash laws.

Be especially careful not to leave animals inside a car during the warm months. On a day that the thermometer hits 105 or 110 degrees, the inside of a closed automobile can quickly reach 150 degrees. Even leaving windows slightly open is not adequate for your pet's safety.

Public Transit

Regional transit in the Phoenix metropolitan area is available within a 500-square mile area. Interconnecting service links transit systems throughout the Valley. Bus routes serve Avondale, Chandler, Fountain Hills, Glendale, Guadalupe, Mesa, Peoria, Scottsdale, Sun City and Tempe. Bus schedules can be obtained at public libraries. Special services are available for handicapped, hearing impaired, and elderly riders. In some areas Dial-A-Ride service is available. Cabs and shuttle services offer alternative transportation. Private shuttle services provide transportation to the airport from many neighborhoods.

For more information about Phoenix bus service, call 253-5000. In Tucson, Sun Tran provides public bus service. Call 792-9222 for schedule and route information.

Airports

Sky Harbor International Airport in Phoenix and Tucson International Airport link Arizonans to nearly every possible destination in the world. Service is also available from Yuma. Arizona is known as a flier's paradise because of the good weather and clear skies. Nearly 200 public and private airports serve the state's aviators.

Media

Newspapers

A good way to get acquainted with the community you're planning to move to is to receive the local newspaper before you arrive. Seven daily newspapers serve the Valley of the Sun: *The Arizona Republic*, *The Phoenix Gazette*, *The Tribune* (Mesa, Chandler and Tempe), *Scottsdale Daily Progress*, *Tempe Daily News* and *Chandler Arizonan*. Tucson has two daily newspapers: *The Tucson Citizen* and the *Arizona Daily Star*. Also of interest may be *Arizona Highways*, *Arizona Senior World* and the *Winter Independent Visitor*.

Television

Phoenix has nine television stations and Tucson has seven. Other cities with stations include Ajo, Flagstaff, Sierra Vista, and Yuma. Cable and relay services enable residents in other parts of the state to receive television signals from Phoenix and Tucson. Several cable companies also service the metro areas.

Radio

Thirty-eight radio stations in Phoenix and another 24 in Tucson offer programming choices for every taste.

Finding a Doctor

There are more than 4,000 physicians to select from in Phoenix and another 1,400 in Tucson. To help you locate the one you need, the Arizona Board of Medical Examiners investigates complaints and compiles records on Arizona physicians. Files are available for public inspection. You may write or visit the office to obtain background information, licensing, letters of concern, and stipulations.

To inquire about an M.D., contact:

> Board of Medical Examiners
> 2001 W. Camelback Rd. #300
> Phoenix, AZ 85015
> 255-3751

To inquire about a D.O., contact:

> Board of Osteopathic Examiners
> 1830 W. Coulter #104
> Phoenix, AZ 85015
> 255-1747

Referrals are also made by the Arizona Medical Association and the Arizona Osteopathic Medical Association. When you contact these Associations, they will provide you with a name of a member of the association in your area with the specialty you are seeking. For more information, contact:

> Arizona Medical Association
> 810 W. Bethany Home Rd.
> Phoenix, AZ 85013
> 246-8901
> Arizona Osteopathic Medical Association
> 5057 E. Thomas Rd.
> Phoenix, AZ 85018
> 840-0460

The Maricopa and Pima County Medical Societies also provide names, specialties and locations of physicians. For more information, contact:

> Maricopa County Medical Society
> 326 E. Coronado
> Phoenix, AZ 85004
> 252-2015

Pima County Medical Society
5199 E. Farness St.
Tucson, AZ 85712
795-7985

In addition, referrals are made by hospitals to doctors on their staffs.

Hospitals in Arizona

The state has ninety hospitals, with major medical facilities in Phoenix and Tucson. There are 37 hospitals in Maricopa County and 15 in Pima County. Good Samaritan Medical Center in Phoenix, St. Joseph's Hospital in Phoenix and Tucson Medical Center each have over 600 beds.

Long Term Health Care

The Arizona Department of Health Services' Office of Long Term Care Services publishes a *Directory of Long Term Health Care Facilities*. It is a complete resource for finding, evaluating, paying for, and monitoring long term health care. The directory gives detailed information on all licensed long term facilities throughout the state. To obtain a free copy of the directory, contact:

Arizona Department of Health Services
Office of Long Term Care

1647 E. Morten #110	400 W. Congress #116
Phoenix, AZ 85020	Tucson, AZ 85701
255-1177	628-6965

The Arizona Health Care Association, a non-profit organization representing long term health care facilities, also provides consumer information and referral services on nursing home care, government financial assistance and locations of facilities. For more information, contact:

Arizona Health Care Association
1440 E. Missouri #215
Phoenix, AZ 85014
265-5331

Social Security

Information about Social Security benefits can be obtained from offices in Flagstaff, Glendale, Mesa, Tucson, Phoenix and Scottsdale, or by phone, at (800) 772-1213.

Veterans Administration

There are three VA hospitals in Arizona, a regional VA office in Phoenix, and veterans' organizations. A statewide toll-free number, (800) 827-1000, can put you in touch with the one you need. In the Phoenix area, call 263-5411.
VA Medical Centers are located:
Phoenix
Seventh St. and Indian School Rd.
Tucson
3601 S. Sixth St.
Prescott
Highway 89 North
The following veterans' organizations have offices adjacent to the VA Regional Center at 3225 N. Central Avenue in Phoenix.

American Legion	American Veterans
277-8052	640-4645
DAV	VFW
277-8215	263-5411
Paralyzed Veterans Association	
244-9168	

Immigration

U.S. Department of Immigration and Naturalization offices
are located at:

2035 N. Central	301 W. Congress
Phoenix, AZ 85004	Tucson, AZ 85701
261-3122	670-4624

Lawyer Referral

The Maricopa County Bar Association operates a Lawyer
Referral Service. Half-hour consultations can be scheduled by
calling 257-4434. There is a $25 fee for this service. In Pima
County, Lawyer Referral Service is available by calling 623-
4625.

Insurance

The State of Arizona publishes premium surveys based on
typical transactions. In a recent survey of automobile
premiums, cost of a particular policy ranged from $246 to
$1,149 in Phoenix. The same driver residing in Tucson might
expect to pay between $202 and $802. The message here is
that you should shop around for the policy that will best suit
your needs. Complaint records are also available from the
insurance department. For more information:

State Department of Insurance
3030 N. Third St. #1100
Phoenix, AZ 85012
In Phoenix Metro Area: 255-5400
Elsewhere in Arizona: (800) 325-2548

Time Zones

Unlike the rest of the nation, Arizona never turns the clock back or ahead. The state is on Mountain Standard Time all year. The only exception is the Navajo nation, which observes Daylight Savings Time.

Area Code

All of Arizona is located in telephone area code 602. Because there has been a shortage of prefixes in the 602 area, you may need to dial the area code for long distance calls, even though they are in the same area code as the one you are calling from.

5

Keeping Your Cool

Skin Protection

In Arizona, the sun is a mixed blessing. While it provides relief from aching joints, psoriasis, acne and supplies Vitamin D, it can also cause wrinkling, premature aging of the skin, leathery and rough skin, sunburn and skin cancer.

Everyone in Arizona is at high risk for developing skin cancer due to the high sun intensity, low latitude, high altitude and clear skies. Arizona has the highest rate of skin cancer in the United States, although more than 95 percent of those cancers can be prevented.

The Arizona Sun Awareness Center at the University of Arizona recommends that you:

- Use a sunscreen with a high Sun Protection Factor. SPF 15 gives maximum protection. SPF 15 will protect most people, even in summer for about two and a half hours. Products are now available with very high SPF numbers and water resistance which can provide daylong protection. Apply sunscreen 30 minutes before going out. The screening agent needs time to react with your skin. Reapply sunscreen if you are out for a long time or if your sunscreen may have washed off. The utraviolet (UV) portion of sunlight (which is the leading cause of skin cancer) cannot be seen or felt. It gets to your skin even on cloudy days and under water. UV rays bounce off water, tile, cement, sand and snow. You need sunscreen even if you wear a hat, cart an umbrella or stand under a tree. Be sure to protect your ears, the backs of your neck, throat, hands, tops of feet and bald spots.

- Avoid the sun between 10 a.m. and 3 p.m. when the sun's rays are strongest. Work or play outdoors earlier or later, whenever you can.
- In addition to applying sunscreen, cover up. Wear long sleeves, long pants, wide brimmed hats, and protective sunglasses that screen out ultraviolet light.
- Know your skin moles and see a doctor when they change.

Light-colored, lightweight clothing that reflects heat and light is your best bet. Natural fibers such as cotton and linen cool better than polyesters. A hat with a wide brim will protect both your eyes and neck. The best choice is a light-colored straw hat with holes for ventilation.

Certain drugs may cause your skin to be particularly sensitive to the sun's ultraviolet rays, including:
- Some antibiotics, such as tetracycline.
- Some diuretics (water pills).
- Some tranquilizers, such as Thorazine and Stelazine.
- Sulfa drugs.
- Some birth control pills and hormones.

This same type of photosensitivity may develop from the use of certain perfumes and artificial sweeteners as well as some cosmetics. Check with your pharmacist or physician to see if any of the medications you take are affected by exposure to the sun.

Managing the Heat

There are several differences which combine to make "desert sunshine" unlike that experienced in other parts of the country. First of all, there's much more of it. The clear desert air and light reflective terrain combine to deliver a more intense dose of sunshine to your skin than in many other parts of the country.

Desert temperatures are hotter and your body begins soaking up heat from the air at 92 degrees. Body temperature will also increase from heat reflected from the ground, direct contact with heated objects, and any work or exercise. Dangerous elevations of body temperature can be caused by absorbing too much heat or by generating it. In the desert, the chances of a person's body reaching dangerous temperature levels must be considered. An elevation of 6 to 8 degrees above the normal for any extended length of time can be fatal.

Dehydration. Your body's major means of cooling itself is by sweating. It is vital that the fluid lost in this way be replaced. Dehydration is a sign that body fluids are being lost. The symptoms include thirst, a tired, lazy feeling, slower body movements, loss of appetite, dizziness and dry mouth. These are signs to drink more water. It is important to begin replacing fluids before symptoms appear. Water is the most effective thirst quencher, better than soda, milk, or fruit juice. Warm or cool water is better than ice cold water. Smoking and alcohol consumption also hasten dehydration.

Symptoms of overheating are serious and call for prompt attention. While heatstroke is more severe than exhaustion, both problems indicate the victim should be promptly removed from the sunlight and medical attention sought.

Heat Exhaustion. Moist, pale, cool skin, muscle cramps and weakness, and a weak pulse are signs of heat exhaustion.

Heatstroke. Headache, nausea, dry, red, and hot skin; strong, fast pulse; convulsions; and unconsciousness are signs of heatstroke. These are signs that the body's cooling system has broken down completely. Get out of the sun and get help quickly.

When temperatures are on the rise, slow down. Pay attention to your body's early warning signs and head for the shade at the first sign of overheating. In very hot weather, cut back on food consumption. Eating increases your body heat and contributes to water loss. Drink plenty of water. In the summer months it's a good idea to keep a supply of drinking water in your car.

Gradual temperature change is better than sudden changes. Shorten the time you are exposed to the heat and watch out for sunburns.

Desert Survival

Neither ruthless nor protective, the desert is a neutral environment, where those who dwell within or visit must adapt their behavior to the naturally-occurring conditions. The greatest desert dangers are fear, ignorance and lack of preparation.

Before venturing out you can reduce your chances of trouble by making sure your car is in good shape. Check tires, belts and carry extra hoses. Be sure the radiator has coolant. To ensure your safety, equip your car with items that will be needed if you should become stranded. Bring one gallon of water per person minimum per day. Water is more important to your survival than anything else. But it is not enough to carry water—you also need to drink it. Thirst is your body's way of warning you that you are losing water faster than you are replacing it. Desert dwellers learn to heed the warning and respond promptly. Other helpful items include extra oil and water for the car, a tire jack, a tow chain, old carpeting with strong backing, and a small box of non-perishable food.

Leave information about your destination and plans to return with friends or relatives. If you become stranded, remain calm, and rely on your common sense. Rescuers recommend that you stay near your car since it is easier to spot than a person. If necessary, you can use items from the car to help search crews find you. Mirrors can be used to signal; trunk tools can be used to dig. Aluminum foil also makes a good signaling device. Carpet can be placed under a wheel that is stuck in sand.

Desert survival is a matter of keeping yourself alive. Search and rescue teams rely heavily on the Civil Air Patrol for assistance. If you are lost, you can assist their efforts by burning the spare tire from your trunk to signal for help. Build a bright evening fire or a smoky daytime fire. Engine oil added to a fire will create heavy smoke, but be extremely careful with fire in the desert for your own safety and to prevent wild fires.

Many organizations offer desert survival classes free or for a minimal charge. If you are unable to attend a class, you can obtain a book on desert survival and read it before departing. Keep a copy in your car.

You can also use newspapers weighted down with rocks to spell out large messages to pilots.

I	Need A Doctor	↑	Going This Way
I I	Need Medicine	L L	All is Well
X	Unable to Proceed	N	No
F	Need Food, Water	Y	Yes
K	Which Way	⌐L	Not Understood
V	Need Firearms	U	Need Map/Compass

Auto Preparedness

Being stranded in summer heat is no picnic. Here are a few things you can do to minimize your risk and make your ride more comfortable.

Replace fan belts and radiator hoses every two years. Rubber dries out in the heat and low humidity of the desert causing it to crack. Check for bulges and cracks at regular intervals. Be sure your car has adequate anti-freeze, which keeps cooling systems from freezing and helps the radiator water dissipate the heat more efficiently. Change the engine oil more frequently (every 3,000 miles) during the summer. Keep the battery clean and filled. Batteries last about three years because of the drying effect of the heat. Replace as soon as you have an indication the battery is weak.

Window tinting can cut out as much as 50 percent of the heat and ultraviolet rays from the sun. If your windows aren't already tinted, metallic film can be installed. Custom mats for the dashboard and rear deck prevent exposed areas from drying out and cracking. Sheepskins are a popular cover for vinyl and leather seats. The air circulates between the fibers and insulates the rider absorbing up to 30 percent of its weight in moisture before feeling wet.

Windshield shades protect the dashboard and reduce the car's inside temperature. There are several styles including fold-up cardboard, and spring-loaded fabric. A good wax job will help reduce paint oxidation protecting the auto's finish. There really *are* more white cars in Arizona than anywhere else. If you drive a black car or other dark-colored vehicle, consider trading it before you move to Arizona. Resale values here are not good for dark cars.

Monsoons and Flash Floods

The hot, dry weather of May and June ushers in the "monsoon" season. When warm moist air flows up from the Gulf of Mexico and is heated by Arizona's strong summer sun, thunderstorms occur. The flow forms a high-pressure system over the northeastern corner of the state and moves in a clockwise direction. The high mountains experience frequent afternoon showers during the season, but the hot and muggy conditions are more pronounced in the southern areas of the state.

Meteorologists use the dew point to define monsoon days. When the average daily dew point is 55 degrees or higher, the day gets tallied as part of the monsoon season. Generally, July through August marks the monsoon season. The storms typically come in the evening or night and can create havoc in areas where there are no storm sewers. Sometimes the storms are rainless displays of lightning.

Heavy, even though brief, rainfall can be followed by flash floods. You are particularly vulnerable in hilly or low terrain. To avoid trouble, stay away from natural streambeds, and other drainage channels during and after rainstorms. Water runs off the higher elevations very rapidly. Never camp on low ground. Know where high ground is and how to get there. Stay out of flooded areas. The National Weather Service has two official warnings regarding flooding:

Flash Flood Watch: Heavy rains may result in flash flooding in the specified area. Be alert and prepared for the possibility of a flood emergency which will require immediate action.

Flash Flood Warning: Flash flooding is occurring or is imminent in specified areas. Move to safe ground immediately.

Dust Storms

Summer winds sometimes pick up dry, loose dirt particles, creating a dust storm. The reddish-brown clouds vary in density, but can limit drivers' visibility.

The Department of Public Safety has a sign system on Interstates 8 and 10 in central Arizona that posts "Dust Storm Alert" messages when such conditions are likely.

If dense blowing dust is observed across a roadway, do not enter the area. If you are caught by a dust storm while driving, reduce the speed of your vehicle and carefully pull off the pavement as far as possible. Avoid stopping on the pavement since this is how most chain reaction accidents happen. Turn off your lights and wait until the dust storm has passed. These dust storms are normally followed by rain, which is a signal that you can resume driving.

Winter Storms

Between November and April, winter storms are common in Arizona's higher elevations. Snow may be falling in northern Arizona while central and southern Arizona is basking in 70 degree temperatures.

When traveling in snow country have plenty of fuel, good tires and be sure your vehicle is in good condition. Carry water, blankets or sleeping bags, warm shoes, clothing, food, flares and a first aid kit. Roads may close completely or be open only to 4-wheel drive vehicles, or those with snowtires or chains. The Department of Public Safety sets up roadblocks to prevent other drivers from using the roads and becoming stranded.

Spiders, Scorpions, Lizards and Snakes

Most bugs you'll meet in Arizona are harmless, and actually serve important roles in keeping nature in balance. Arizona's hot, dry, climate frees residents of many of the bug problems, such as water bugs and roaches, that you'll find in humid areas. You'll also find few rodent problems here. There are a few natives, however, that should be approached cautiously and medical help should be sought immediately if you are bitten.

Black Widows. Shaped like a globe, this spider is black and shiny with red or orange hourglass shaped markings on its stomach. Its distinctive, strong, irregular-shaped web makes it easy to identify.

Brown Spiders. Often found hiding in closets, under firewood, and under the sink, this spider is about the size of a nickel or a quarter. It has a violin-shaped mark on the back of its head and chest region and is light tan or brown.

Scorpions. Only one of the 15 varieties of scorpions found in Arizona is very dangerous. It is about one and a half inches long and has nearly transparent skin with slender pincers, and a slender tail.

Lizards. Common and for the most part harmless little creatures, lizards love to sunbathe and climb block walls. The only poisonous species is the gila monster. It is easily recognizable by its size. About a foot long with a heavy tail and beadlike skin, it is black with shades of orange and pink.

Snakes. There are a number of poisonous snakes in the desert, but very few deaths occur from snakebites. Most cases are the result of the victim attempting to handle or catch the snake.

Rattlesnakes have a large triangular head and usually have a number of rattles on their tail. If you plan to be outdoors frequently, consult a first aid manual to be sure you are up-to-date on the latest techniques for treating bites.

6

Just for the Fun of It

The Great Outdoors

Warm temperatures, dry air, and gorgeous scenery lure desert dwellers outdoors. A variety of life thrives within the desert. You'll find hundreds of native plants, birds, mammals, reptiles, and amphibians. Of all the wildlife species found in North America, 60 percent reside in Arizona and some are found only in this state. Not counting the migratory birds, there are some 400 different species of birds that dwell in the state. The bird watching is unbeatable at Madera Canyon in the Santa Rita Mountains, in the Chiricahua Mountains, and the MileHi/Ramsey Canyon Preserve near Sierra Vista.

Mileposts

To make getting around just a bit easier, you'll find that Arizona is one of the few states in which all state highways have reference markers. The markers can be found a mile apart two feet from the right shoulder of the road.

If you have an accident, mechanical problem, run out of gas, or are unable to proceed, you can use the mileposts to determine your exact location. They are also handy for giving directions to someone you are planning to meet, finding trailheads, etc. If you get into trouble, the Division of Motor Vehicle recommends you note the number of the route you are travelling, your direction, and approximate distance to the next milepost. Then use the most accessible means of communication to relay your message to the Department of Public Safety.

Maps

A state highway map is available at no charge courtesy of *Arizona Highways* magazine. It is available from the Arizona Highways office, state inspection stations, as well as Chamber of Commerce offices. For more information, contact:

Arizona Highways
2039 W. Lewis Ave.
Phoenix, AZ 85009
258-6641

Many other individual and county wall maps are also available from the Department of Transportation. To obtain a free brochure, contact:

Arizona Department of Transportation
Engineering Records Services
206 S. 17th Ave., Room 134A
Phoenix, AZ 85007

Retail map outlets can also supply you with a wide variety of topographic, geologic and city maps.

The fishing is always great in the White Mountains.

Hunting, Fishing, and Boating

The Arizona Game and Fish Department oversees hunting, fishing, and boating in the state. One outdoor guide to Arizona fishing and hunting promises, "Someplace in Arizona, every day of the year, the weather is good, the fishing is fine, and some hunting season is under way."

Variety and abundance characterize the state's hunting and fishing opportunities. The majority of the estimated 1,200 species of wildlife found in Arizona are unhunted, including several species which are considered endangered or in need of protection. Protected species include elk, bighorn sheep, buffalo, eagles, deer, antelope, mountain lion, bear, turkey, javelina, beaver, goose, and raptors.

The Game and Fish Department is funded through license fees and permit tags. Land in Arizona is owned or managed by five different agencies; each has its own access rules. Generally, U.S. Forest Service, Bureau of Land Management, and State lands are open for hunting. National parks and monuments and state parks are not.

Anyone over the age of 14 is required to have a license to take fish in the state. Trout fishing requires the purchase of an additional stamp. Residents may obtain fishing regulations at outlets where licenses are sold, and non-residents may obtain regulations by writing to the Game and Fish Department.

Anyone 14 years old or older may hunt wildlife in Arizona with a hunting license. No state license, tag, or permit is required to hunt or fish on any Indian reservation in this state, however, reservation restrictions do apply. Hunting regulations are complex and vary considerably by game and locale.

With more than 160,000 registered boats in this state, boating is a popular recreational activity. *The Arizona Boating Guide* (available from the Arizona Game and Fish Department), gives a complete description of the state's boating regulations. Every watercraft operated, moored, or anchored on the waterways of Arizona must be numbered. The owner must file an application with the Game and Fish Department and the numbers must be displayed on each side of the bow along with the current registration decal issued by the department.

Major boating areas are found on the Colorado River and the lakes created by its many dams. Under normal conditions any well-equipped and seaworthy craft with adequate freeboard may be safely used. Stay alert for changing wind and weather conditions and inquire about local conditions before setting out. For more specific information about hunting, fishing, or boating, contact:

> Arizona Game and Fish Department
> 2222 W. Greenway Rd.
> Phoenix, AZ 85023
> 942-3000

Camping

Descriptive information about more than 250 campgrounds under the jurisdiction of the U.S. Forest Service, U.S. National Park Service, Bureau of Land Management, Arizona State Parks, Indian reservations and those operated by county and local governments is available from the Office of Tourism. For information, contact:

Arizona Office of Tourism
1100 W. Washington St.
Phoenix, AZ 85007
542-8687 or (800) 842-8257

To maintain the delicate balance of nature, keep campfires small and under control. Carry out whatever you carry in. Camp away from water holes or areas used by wildlife and livestock. Never camp in a dry wash or an area exposed to flash flooding. Check specific regulations before entering an area, since many vary by season.

Rock Hounding

Even the untrained eye can see there are a lot of rocks in Arizona. If you can tell pyrite from peridot, you're in for an adventure. An abundance of rock fields, many loaded with desirable specimens, can be found throughout the state.

Copper and gold have long played an important role in the development of the region. One of Arizona's prime pioneer gold-producing sections is the Golden Triangle located between Phoenix and Prescott and formed by US89, AZ69, and I-17. Gold dust and even small nuggets are found in this region.

Because of their value as gemstones, other minerals have also played a role in the state's economy, including turquoise, peridot, amethyst, opal, and fire agate. Arizona also has abundant supplies of tourmaline, quartz, jasper, and petrified wood.

Each February, rock hounds gather at Tucson and Quartzsite. Watch for the Tucson Gem & Mineral Show and the Quartzsite Pow Wow & Mineral Show. Geologists, prospectors, appraisers, gem retailers, and hobbyists from six continents and all across the United States meet in Tucson to attend special seminars, workshops and trade wares in what's billed as the largest show of its kind. At Quartzsite, you can expect 500 dealers and 100,000 rock hounds for the trade-a-thon.

Hiking

A great way to see the state is on foot. Some of Arizona's best sites can only be reached this way. Hiking clubs schedule weekly outings and rate their hikes according to difficulty. In just the Tonto National Forest alone there are 875 miles of trails. Add to that the other national forests, state parks, etc., and you'll probably always have a trail to conquer.

There are several excellent trail books available if you prefer to hike on your own. A trip to a nearby hiking and camping supply store will put you in touch with local organizations and point you to the hiking guidebooks.

Golf

Arizona has long been a golfer's paradise. The year-round season has made the state a favorite of duffers and pros alike. You'll find traditional style as well as challenging desert courses here. The Arizona Golf Association lists more than 150 courses. If you're interested in sampling what the state has to offer, you can purchase your own copy of the non-profit

AGA's *Directory of Arizona Golf Courses*. For current price and order information, contact:

> Arizona Golf Association
> 7226 N. 16th St. #200
> Phoenix, AZ 85020
> 944-3035

Several professional golf tournaments are held in the state each year giving spectators ample opportunity to take note of how the pros do it so well. The Phoenix Open is held at the Tournament Players Course in Scottsdale each January; and in October the PGA stops in Tucson for the Seiko Tucson Match Play at the Randolph Park North Golf Course. The LPGA tour spends part of March in Arizona, with a week in Tucson and then on to the Moon Valley Country Club in north Phoenix for the Turquoise Classic. The Senior PGA also often makes an Arizona stop.

Tennis

Bright, sunny days and crisp, clear air are the natural setting for a set or two of tennis. There are courts galore throughout the metropolitan areas including many topnotch public courts. Tucson and Scottsdale each have well over 200 public tennis courts and Phoenix boasts an additional 350 public courts. The climate favors hard-surface courts.

Superstars regularly swing into action with major national junior, senior, and pro tournaments each season as well as frequent charitable exhibitions by pro players. Several pros make their home here and visitors come to improve their game at local tennis resorts. Whatever your skill level, you'll find courts and challenges to match.

Baseball

Each spring the Cactus League gears up for a month of spring training. In the pre-season, all seats are up close with plenty of opportunity to catch a fly ball or get an autograph. To receive ticket information write to the team's main office and ask to be placed on the spring training mailing list. Teams training in Arizona include:

California Angels
Gene Autry Park
4125 E. McKellips Rd., Mesa

San Francisco Giants
Scottsdale Stadium
7408 E. Osborn Rd., Scottsdale

Chicago Cubs
HoHoKam Park
1235 N. Center St., Mesa

Milwaukee Brewers
Compadre Stadium
1425 W. Ocotillo Rd., Chandler

Cleveland Indians
Randolph Park
900 S. Randolph Way, Tucson

Seattle Mariners
Tempe Diablo Stadium
2525 S. 48th St., Tempe

Oakland A's
Phoenix Stadium
5999 E. Van Buren St., Phoenix

San Diego Padres
Desert Sun Stadium
Avenue A at 35th St., Yuma

In the summer, the Class AAA Phoenix Firebirds and the Tucson Toros take to the field. The Firebirds play at Phoenix Municipal Stadium at 5999 E. Van Buren Street in Phoenix while the Toros are at home at Hi Corbett Field, 900 S. Randolph Way in Tucson.

Skiing

Even though most of us think of Arizona as a hotspot, there are four major snow ski areas in the state, allowing city dwellers to be on the slopes in a matter of hours.

The southern-most ski area in the United States is at Mount Lemmon in the Catalina Mountains, just an hour's drive from Tucson. In the Flagstaff area you'll find Fairfield Snowbowl on the slopes of the San Francisco Peaks and Bill Williams Mountain. Sunrise, located in the White Mountains, is owned and operated by the White Mountain Apache Tribe. Cross country skiing is plentiful in the north with popular trails near Mormon Lake, Greer, and Springerville.

Basketball

The NBA's Phoenix Suns take on challengers at the America West Arena in downtown Phoenix. For a schedule and ticket information, call 379-7867.

Racing

Whatever your taste in excitement, you'll find it in Arizona. There's a full season of Thoroughbred racing with pari-mutuel betting from October through May at Turf Paradise/Arizona Downs in Phoenix. The track is located at 19th Avenue and Bell Road. For information call 942-1101. At Prescott Downs, the season runs from May to September. For more information, call 445-0220.

Greyhounds race at Greyhound Park with locations in Phoenix, Apache Junction, Tucson, and Yuma. Seasons vary by location.

The roar of internal combustion engines pierces the air outside Tolleson at Phoenix International Raceway, in Phoenix at Manzanita Speedway, and in Chandler at Firebird International.

Christmas in the Desert

Northerners sometimes wonder what Christmas is like without snow. Newcomers who have been here for a short while respond that they've never before felt so much holiday spirit as they have discovered in the Southwest. A big reason for that is the the traditional Mexican luminarias which light up city streets, desert gardens, and city mountains.

A luminaria is made by placing a votive candle in sand in the base of a paper bag. When the candle is lit, the bag casts glowing shadows. Spectacular displays can be found on Christmas Eve in Phoenix's Moon Valley and Tucson's Winterhaven neighborhoods. Earlier in the month the Desert Botanical Garden lights its walkways for a holiday evening and on another December eve the trail up Squaw Peak, Phoenix's most hiked mountain, is ablaze with luminarias.

At Page, boats of all sizes, decked with lights to look like floating Christmas trees, slowly cruise Lake Powell for the Festival of Lights procession.

The lack of snowfall in southern Arizona makes it much easier to put up the Christmas lights and Arizonans do it with gusto. The scarcity of coniferous trees doesn't stop anyone. Saguaros, ocotillos, and prickly pears get into the act, as do the palm, orange, and lemon trees. You'll even see tumbleweed snowmen.

Places to Visit

Arizona offers an endless variety of natural wonders from the dewdrops glistening on a spider web in early morning to the self-propelled roadrunner who glides across city streets. The state has more national parks and monuments than any other. Add to those a marvelous assortment of state parks, marginhelper

The North Rim Lodge offers visitors a new perspective on the Canyon.

scenic byways, city and county parks and you'll never run out of things to see.

Grand Canyon National Park

Location: South Rim—At Williams, take AZ 64 n. 58 mi. North Rim—45 mi. s. of Jacob Lake on AZ 67

This is nature at her most impressive. The Colorado River has whittled rock patterns thousands of feet deep to build kaleidoscopes of color. After billions of years of work the river has left spires, precipes and plateaus rising dramatically from the canyon floor. The images are so vast and spectacular that people come from all over the world just to stand at the edge and view the power of wind, water and time.

At the Canyon, you can ride rapids, hike trails, ride a mule train or helicopter across. There are campgrounds and lodges. Visitors are encouraged to make reservations. In the busy summer months, facilities are booked far in advance. There is an admission fee to enter the park.

The visitor count has steadily edged upward to four million per year, 90 percent of whom visit the South Rim, which is open year-round. The North Rim, with cooler temperatures, more rainfall, trees and wildflowers also offers inviting panoramas with less congestion.

For more information:
> Grand Canyon National Park
> P.O. Box 129
> Grand Canyon, AZ 86023
> 638-7888

For lodging information:
> Grand Canyon National Park Lodges
> P.O. Box 699
> Grand Canyon, AZ 86023
> 638-2401

Oak Creek Canyon

Location: From Phoenix, take I-17 n. to AZ 179 (Exit 298), turn l. and proceed another 14 mi.

The red walls of Oak Creek Canyon soar 2,500 feet in places. The views are from the canyon floor where a paved road follows Oak Creek. Each year 2.5 million visitors come to see colorful, ever-changing patterns of light and shadow play on the steep walls of the 16-mile canyon. For the adventuresome, Schnebly Hill Road, a rustic yet scenic drive, provides magnificent views from an awesome perspective. A more sedate drive through the canyon on AZ 89A leads to Slide Rock State Park, where nature has carved a natural slide in the rock of the creek bed. A favorite with hikers is the West Fork Trail. The trailhead is between mileposts 384 and 385 along US 89A.

Below Oak Creek is Sedona, long considered an artist colony and home to some of the West's finest art galleries. There's also market square shopping at Tlaquepaque.

Cathedral Rock, near Red Rock Loop Crossing west of Sedona.

Activities in and around Oak Creek include swimming, fishing, hunting, hiking, camping, photography, and bird watching. The Red Rock State Park just west of Sedona provides additional public access to some of the country's most spectacular scenery. For more information:

Sedona-Oak Creek Chamber of Commerce
P.O. Box 478
Sedona, AZ 86336
282-7722

Canyon de Chelly National Monument

Location: Just e. of Chinle in n. central Arizona

One way to tell how new you are to the state is how you pronounce the name of this national monument. This 26-mile stretch of rare beauty is located in the heart of the Navajo reservation. Sandstone walls rise a thousand feet from the canyon floor. Within the canyons, centuries-old Anasazi

Indian ruins from the Pueblo Period (1100-1300 A.D) are preserved. Don't miss Spider Rock, one of the most extraordinary monoliths in all of Indian country. It rises 832 feet into sky where Canyon de Chelly meets Monument Canyon.

The National Park Service administers the area, protects the ruins, and manages visitor access. Navajo families still summer on the canyon floor.

For more information:

        Canyon de Chelly National Monument
        P.O. Box 588
        Chinle, AZ 86503
        674-5436

        Navajoland Tourism Office
        P.O. Box 663
        Window Rock, AZ 86515
        871-6436

Mogollon Rim

Location: A 300 mi. expanse from New Mexico into central and eastern Arizona.

The Mogollon Rim separates the plateau country of the north from the low country of the south. The near vertical 2,000 foot drop is covered with timber and rock. Zane Grey lived along the Rim and wrote for many years using the neighborhood as the setting for several novels.

The General Crook Trail, now known as U.S. Forest Service Road 300, begins on AZ 260 near Christopher Creek and follows the rim for about 30 miles to Strawberry, where it leads to AZ 87. There are plenty of stops and breathtaking lookouts along the way.

Activities along the rim include fishing, hunting, boating, water skiing, hiking, backpacking, camping, photography, and horseback riding.

For more information:

    Tonto National Forest
    P.O. Box 5348
    Phoenix, AZ 85010
    225-5200

Petrified Forest National Park

Location: 25 mi. e. of Holbrook on I-40

This 160 million-year-old forest contains the largest find of petrified wood in the world. President Theodore Roosevelt designated the area as a national monument in 1906, making it illegal to remove even the tiniest sliver of petrified wood or any other fossil, archaeological relic, or living plant. Those regulations are strictly enforced.

The Painted Desert, a rainbow of naturally-colored landforms that change with the day's light is located in the park's northern quadrant. In 1985, the skeleton of a 225 million-year-old dinosaur, the oldest ever found, was unearthed at the park.

Activities here include sightseeing, photography, picnicking, hiking, and casual walking along park trails. Overnight pack trips are allowed with permits. A 28-mile road winds through this showcase of ancient history.

For more information:

    Petrified Forest National Park
    Holbrook, AZ 86028
    524-6228

Meteor Crater

Location: 40 mi. e. of Flagstaff and 20 mi. w. of Winslow on I-40

About 20,000 years ago a nickel-iron meteor traveling over 45,000 miles per hour created this gigantic crater. When it struck the earth, the meteor destroyed all life within 100 miles. The crater, which is more than three miles in circumference and 570 feet deep, was the training facility for astronauts preparing for moon walks. The Museum of Astrogeology at the site features earth and space science displays. There is an admission charge.

For more information:

> Meteor Crater Enterprises
> 603 N. Beaver St. Ste C
> Flagstaff, AZ 86001
> 774-8350

Monument Valley

Location: From Kayenta take US 163 n. 24 mi., turn right 3.5 mi. to the Visitor's Center

You're likely to think you've been here before, since advertisers love to perch cars on Monument Valley's ledges. Hollywood film director John Ford used this setting near the Utah border for many Western classics, some of which starred the legendary John Wayne. More recently it was seen in the *Back to the Future* movies. Eroded buttes, plateaus and monuments tower over the valley in brilliant reds, rusts and ruddy browns. The monuments were formed by upheaval followed by centuries of wind and water erosion. Owned and managed by the Navajo people, jeep tours led by Navajo guides enable visitors to see the entire valley.

Monument Valley

For more information:
> Monument Valley Park Headquarters
> Box 93
> Monument Valley, AZ 84563
> Navajoland Tourism Office
> P.O. Box 663
> Window Rock, AZ 86515
> 871-6436

Lake Powell

Location: Just n. of Page

Although most of Lake Powell is actually in Utah, the southern entrance to the Glen Canyon National Recreation Area is in Arizona. Fire-red rocks, cliffs and sandy beaches surround nearly 200 miles of turquoise water enclosed by 2,000-shoreline miles. Lake Powell is the second largest man-made lake in the United States. Glen Canyon Dam towers 710 feet and was one of the largest construction projects ever undertaken.

You can see Rainbow Bridge National Monument by boat or hike in on a rugged, but beautiful, 14-mile trail. The impressive arch is 309-feet high and 278-feet wide.

Lake activities include houseboating, skiing, fishing, hiking, backpacking, photography, and bird watching.

For more information:

Glen Canyon National Recreation Area
P.O. Box 1507
Page, AZ 86040
645-8200

Page/Lake Powell Chamber of Commerce
P.O. Box 727
Page, AZ 86040
645-2741

Heard Museum

Location: 22 East Monte Vista Rd., Phoenix (3 blocks n. of McDowell Rd and 1 block e. of Central Ave.)

The world-renowned Heard Museum houses the world's definitive exhibit of Southwest culture, as well as changing exhibits of contemporary sculpture and paintings by Native American artists. Since the private, non-profit museum opened in 1929, more than 75,000 items have been catalogued, including the world's finest and largest collection of Hopi Kachina dolls.

An authentic Navajo hogan, an Apache wickiup, and a Hopi corn grinding room were built for the exhibit by Native Americans. Native Americans arts and crafts are sold at the gift shop. In addition to traditional items such as Kachina dolls, pottery, basketry, jewelry and textiles, you'll find contemporary paintings, graphics and sculpture by today's emerging Native American artists. There is an admission fee.

For more information:

The Heard Museum
22 Monte Vista Rd.
Phoenix, AZ 85004
252-8848

Arizona-Sonora Desert Museum

Location: 2021 N. Kinney Rd., Tucson (Take the Gates Pass exit w. from I-10, 14 mi.)

The drive to the museum passes through one of the world's most magnificent saguaro forests. The museum itself features living animals and plants of the Sonoran region found in Arizona, Sonora, Baja, California, and Mexico. Frequently cited as one of the most unusual zoos in the United States, you'll find every imaginable desert plant, animal, reptile, and bird here—more than 200 animals and 300 living desert plants in natural habitats. There is an admission fee.

For more information:

Arizona-Sonora Desert Museum
2021 N. Kinney Rd.
Tucson, AZ 85743
883-1380

Desert Botanical Garden

Location: 1201 N. Galvin Parkway, Phoenix (in Papago Park between Van Buren St. and McDowell Rd.)

The Desert Botanical Gardens features plants from deserts all over the world. Each year 100,000 visitors come to see the 2,500 plant species exhibited here. A Wildflower Hotline is in operation in the spring months with an up-to-date report on where to see the desert in bloom. Two evenings each December the garden paths are lined with luminarias for a holiday walk. There is an admission fee.

For more information:
Desert Botanical Garden
1201 N. Galvin Pkwy.
Phoenix, AZ 85008
941-1225

Boyce Thompson Southwestern Arboretum

Location: 3 mi. w. of Superior between Florence Junction and Superior on US 60-70 (60 mi. from Phoenix)

The Arizona State Parks, the University of Arizona, and the non-profit Arboretum corporation manage 1,076 acres which shelter 1,500 species of desert plants from the United States and around the world. The arboretum also has geological gardens and many birds and animals in their natural habitat. Hiking trails of varying lengths allow visitors to saunter through the gardens at their own pace. There is an admission fee.

For more information:
Boyce Thompson Southwestern Arboretum
P.O. Box AB
Superior, AZ 85273
689-2811

Phoenix Zoo

Location: 5801 E. Van Buren St., Phoenix (Enter from Galvin Parkway in Papago Park)

The largest privately-owned, self-supporting zoo in the country, the zoo has 350 animal species. Unlike most other zoos, animals are grouped within the 125-acre grounds according to origins. Tropical rainforests, mountains, grasslands, woodlands, and desert areas provide habitats for the animals. There is an admission fee.

For more information:
> Phoenix Zoo
> 5810 E. Van Buren St.
> Phoenix, AZ 85008
> 273-7771

London Bridge

Location: Lake Havasu City

In a magnificent feat of modern engineering, developer Robert McCullough paid $2.5 million to purchase this bridge and then paid more than double the purchase price to dismantle it and ship it from England to Arizona. The bridge was reassembled on dry land and a mile-long channel was excavated beneath it.

The bridge and its adjacent English village are the focal point of a multi-million dollar resort complex of shops, restaurants, and lodging facilities.

For more information:
> Lake Havasu Area Visitor & Convention Bureau
> 1930 Mesquite Ave., Suite 3
> Lake Havasu City, AZ 86403
> 453-3444

San Xavier del Bac Mission

Location: 9 mi. sw. of Tucson (Take I-19 s. to Valencia Rd., turn w. on Mission Rd. and follow the signs.)

From a distance you'll spot the twin-towered structure frequently called "The White Dove of the Desert." The 200-year-old mission is located at a site missionary Father Kino visited in 1692. The original structure was destroyed by Apache warriors and rebuilt in the 18th century by the Franciscans. The architecture combines Moorish, Byzantine, and late Mexican styles and is considered one of the finest examples of mission architecture in the United States. A registered national historic landmark since 1963, the mission is still in use and is the spiritual center for the San Xavier Indian Reservation. Bring your camera.

For more information:

Tohono O'Odham Tribal Council
P.O. Box 837
Sells, AZ 85634
383-2221

Mission San Xavier del Bac, near Tucson.

Mexico

Ever since 1540 when Francisco Vasquez de Coronado crossed the Mexican mountains into what is now Arizona the fascination of the natives of one country with the culture and traditions of the other country has persisted. The 230-mile Arizona-Mexico border has six places to cross, the most popular of which is Nogales, just 63 miles south of Tucson.

American citizens do not need visas to visit border communities if they do not plan to travel more than three miles below the border or stay more than 72 hours. You can also park your car and walk across the border. If you are going farther or are planning an extended stay, you will need a Tourist Card and an Automobile Permit. To obtain those, identification such as a birth certificate, voter's registration card, passport or military identification card that shows your place of birth, or a typewritten notarized affidavit showing your name, place of birth, and citizenship is required.

Tourist Cards are available at the border or at:

Mexican Consulate
553 S. Stone Ave.
Tucson, AZ 85701
882-5595

Most U.S. auto insurance policies *do not* cover driving in Mexico. Mexican auto insurance can be obtained near the border.

Mexican shopping markets and restaurants appeal to many visitors. In Nogales, Calle Obregon is the main shopping area, but you'll also be pleased with the Calle Elias near the Morley Street border crossing, just east of the gate.

Shoppers favor handicrafts which include serapes from Saltillo and Oaxaca, pottery from Puebla, leather wallets from Jalisco, guitars from Michoacan, as well as vanilla from Papantla, Veracruz. Tequila, Kahlua, and Mexican rum and brandy often make the return trip with visitors. Check local prices before you go, so you'll know a bargain when you see one. Only one quart of liquor per adult can be brought back.

While the peso is standard currency, you'll have no trouble paying in American dollars near the border. You can bring $400 of merchandise back into the United States duty-free.

Indian Reservations

A visit to an Indian reservation can be a memorable Arizona experience. Most tribes welcome visitors and maintain information centers to be of assistance. Keep in mind that visitors are expected to honor the customs and culture of the people whose reservation they are visiting.

Ak-Chin Reservation

Location: 56 mi. s. of Phoenix in Pinal County
Size: 21,840 acres
Tribe: Papago-Pima
Known For: Basketry
Attractions: St. Francis Church Feast, October 4, Tribal Election Barbecue, the second Saturday in January
For more information:
Ak-Chin Indian Community
42507 W. Peters and Nall Rd.
Maricopa, AZ 85239
568-2227

Camp Verde Reservation

Location: 94 mi. n. of Phoenix in Yavapai County
Size: 653 acres

Tribe: Apache
Known For: Basketry
Attractions: Yavapai-Apache Information Center, Indian Ruins, Montezuma Castle National Monument, Montezuma's Well, hunting, hiking and fishing
For more information:
Yavapai-Apache Indian Community
P.O. Box 1188
Camp Verde, AZ 86322
567-3649

Cocopah East and West Reservations

Location: 211 mi. sw. of Phoenix in Yuma County
Size: 6,009 acres
Tribe: Cocopahs
Known for: Beadwork
Attraction: Heritage Art Museum
For more information:
Cocopah Tribal Council
Bin "G"
Somerton, AZ 85350
627-2102

Colorado River Reservation

Location: 189 mi. w. of Phoenix in Yuma County
Size: 269,918 acres (parts in California)
Tribes: Chemehevi, Mohave
Known For: Basketry, beadwork, and Indian motif wall clocks.
Attractions: 100 miles of river frontage, Lake Moovala speedboat races, All-Indian Rodeo, Indian Day Celebration, Arts and Crafts Center and Museum, dove and quail hunting, fishing, picnicking and water sports

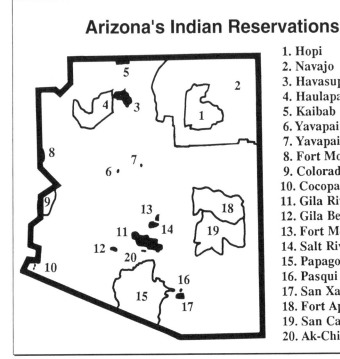

Arizona's Indian Reservations

1. Hopi
2. Navajo
3. Havasupai
4. Haulapai
5. Kaibab
6. Yavapai Prescott
7. Yavapai Clarkdale
8. Fort Mohave
9. Colorado River
10. Cocopah
11. Gila River
12. Gila Bend
13. Fort McDowell
14. Salt River
15. Papago
16. Pasqui Yaqui
17. San Xavier
18. Fort Apache
19. San Carlos
20. Ak-Chin

For more information:
   Colorado River Indian Tribes
   Rt. 1, Box 23-B
   Parker, AZ 85344
   669-9211

Fort Apache Reservation

Location: 194 mi. ne. of Phoenix in Apache, Gila and Navajo counties
Size: 1,664,984 acres
Tribe: Apache
Known For: Basketry ("Burden Baskets") and beadwork
Attractions: Apache Sunrise Resort, Apache Cultural Center,

Annual Rodeo and Fair (Labor Day Weekend), ceremonials, camping, fishing, skiing, horseback riding, hiking, big game hunts, river and river running
> For more information:
> > White Mountain Apache Tribe
> > P.O. Box 700
> > Whiteriver, AZ 85941
> > 338-4346

Fort McDowell Reservation

Location: 36 mi. ne. of Phoenix in Maricopa County
Size: 24,680 acres
Tribe: Apache
Known For: Basketry
Attractions: Camping, fishing, tubing, small game hunting, Ba'Ja bingo, Victory Celebration (mid-November)
> For more information:
> > Mohave-Apache Tribal Council
> > P.O. Box 17779
> > Fountain Hills, AZ 85268
> > 837-5121

Fort Mohave Reservation

Location: 236 mi. nw. of Phoenix in Mohave County
Size: 22,820 acres (parts in California and Nevada)
Tribe: Mohave
Known for: Basketry and beadwork
Attractions: Fishing, dove and quail hunting, picnicking, camping, water sports, Fort Mohave Days (October)

For more information:
>   Fort Mohave Tribe
>   500 Merrimam Ave.
>   Needles, CA 92363
>   (619) 326-4591

Fort Yuma Reservation

Location: 185 mi. sw. of Phoenix in Yuma County
Size: 43,581 acres (parts in California)
Tribe: Yuma
Known For: Beadwork and artifacts
Attractions: Colorado River, fishing, picnicking, water sports, camping, Fort Yuma Quechan Museum, Fourth of July celebration, Indian Day (late September)
>   For more information:
>   Quechan Tribe
>   P.O. Box 11352
>   Yuma, AZ 85364
>   (619) 572-0213

Gila River Reservation

Location: 40 mi. s. of Phoenix in Maricopa and Pinal counties
Size: 372,000 acres
Tribes: Papago, Pima
Known For: Pima basketry and Maricopa pottery
Attractions: Gila River Arts and Crafts Center, Gila Heritage Village and Museum, Firebird Lake and Water Sports Marina, Mul-Cha-Tha (Gathering of the People), Rodeo and Miss Gila River Pageant, St. John's Mission Fair

For more information:
   Gila River Community
   P.O. Box 97
   Sacaton, AZ 85247
   963-4323

Havasupai Reservation

Location: 438 mi. nw. of Phoenix in Coconino County
Size: 188,077 acres
Tribe: Havasupai
Known For: Basketry and beadwork
Attractions: To reach the reservation you must take an eight-mile trail from Hilltop to Supai by pack mules, on foot, or by helicopter. The people of the "Blue-Green Waters" are located at the bottom of Havasupai Canyon, a tributary of the Grand Canyon.
   For more information:
      Havasupai Tribe
      P.O. Box 10
      Supai, AZ 86435
      448-2961

Hopi Reservation

Location: 323 mi. ne. of Phoenix in Coconino and Navajo counties
Size: 1,561,213 acres
Tribe: Hopi
Known for: Kachina dolls, basketry, pottery, plaques, silver crafts
Attractions: Cultural Center, Ceremonials

For more information:
Hopi Tribe
P.O. Box 123
Kyakotsmovi, AZ 86039
734-2441

Hualapai Reservation

Location: 252 mi. nw. of Phoenix in Coconino, Yavapai and Mohave counties
Size: 992,463 acres
Tribe: Hualapai
Known for: Basketry, dolls
Attractions: Camping, hiking, hunting, fishing, white water trips on the Colorado River
For more information:
Hualapai Tribal Council
P.O. Box 179
Peach Springs, AZ 86434
769-2216

Kaibab-Paiute Reservation

Location: 350 mi. n. of Phoenix in Mohave County
Size: 120,827 acres
Tribe: Kaibab-Paiute
Known for: Coiled, shallow "Wedding Baskets"
Attractions: Pipe Springs National Monument, Museum
For more information:
Kaibab-Paiute Tribal Council
Pipe Springs Rt.
Fredonia, AZ 86022
643-7245

Navajo Reservation

Location: 260 mi. ne. of Phoenix in Apache, Coconino, and Navajo counties
Size: 14,775,068 acres
Tribe: Navajo
Known for: Blanket and tapestry weaving, silver and basketry
Attractions: Seven Wonders of the Navajo Nation—Monument Valley, Canyon de Chelly, Little Colorado River Gorge, Grand Falls, Rainbow Bridge, Betatakin, Window Rock—Four Corners, ceremonials, Rodeo & Art Fair, shops, camping, hunting, fishing and hiking
For more information:
> Navajoland Tourism
> P.O. Box 653
> Window Rock, AZ 86515
> 871-6436

Pascua-Yaqui Reservation

Location: 135 mi. sw. of Phoenix in Pima County
Size: 895 acres
Tribe: Yaqui
Known for: Deer dance statues, children's paintings
Attractions: Easter Ceremonial and September Recognition Ceremonials
For more information:
> Pascua-Yaqui Tribe
> 7474 S. Camino de Oeste
> Tucson, AZ 85746
> 883-2838

Salt River Reservation

Location: 15 mi. ne. of Phoenix in Maricopa County
Size: 55,807 acres
Tribe: Pima, Maricopa
Known for: Basketry and pottery
Attractions: Hoo-hoogam Ki Museum, tubing, camping, and picnicking on the Salt River
    For more information:
           Salt River Pima-Maricopa Community
           10000 E. Osborn Rd.
           Scottsdale, AZ 85256
           941-7277

San Carlos Reservation

Location: 115 mi. ne. of Phoenix in Gila and Graham counties
Size: 1,826,541 acres
Tribe: Apache
Known for: Basketry, beadwork, and peridot jewelry
Attractions: San Carlos Lake: fishing, camping and hunting, Seneca Park, Point of Pine, Cassadore Springs
    For more information:
           San Carlos Apache Tribe
           P.O. Box 0
           San Carlos, AZ 85550
           475-2361
    Hunting and fishing information:
           Game and Fish Dept.
           P.O. Box 0
           San Carlos, AZ 85550
           475-2343

Tohono O'odham Reservation

Location: 136 mi. s. of Phoenix in Maricopa, Pinal, and Pima counties
Size: 17,704 acres
Tribe: Papago
Known for : Basketry and pottery
Attractions: Kitt Peak National Observatory, Ventana Canyon, Forteleza Ruins, Mission San Xavier Del Bac and Rodeo & Fair
> For more information:
> > Tohono O'odham Tribe
> > P.O. Box 837
> > Sells, AZ 85634
> > 383-2221

Tonto-Apache Reservation

Location: 94 mi. ne. of Phoenix in Gila County
Size: 85 acres
Tribe: Apache
Known for: Basketry and beadwork
Attractions: Hiking and picnicking
> For more information:
> > Tonto-Apache Tribe
> > Tonto-Apache Reservation No. 30
> > Payson, AZ 85541
> > 474-5000

Yavapai-Prescott Reservation

Location: *103 mi. nw. of Phoenix in Yavapai County*
Size: 1,399 acres
Tribe: Yavapai
Known for: Basketry
Attractions: Yavapai-Apache Visitor's Center, hiking and picnicking
> For more information:
>> Yavapai-Prescott Tribal Council
>> 530 E. Merritt
>> Prescott, AZ 86301
>> 445-8790

While this only scratches the surface of Arizona attractions, it will get you started. As you travel you can expand the list to include many less well-known spots. You'll find more details on things to see and do in and around the metropolitan Phoenix area in *Destination: Phoenix.*

Back to Work

Thousands of adults are redefining "retirement" to suit their own needs. For some, retirement means merely a change to a new life activity rather than a complete abandonment of work.

Several factors now contribute to the increased interest in work as a retirement activity, including healthier lifestyles, opportunities for retiring at an earlier age, the recognition that work is good for you both physically and psychologically, and the desire to supplement sources of retirement income.

Recently workers who accepted early retirement offers from their employers were studied. Eighty-five percent were happy with their decision. The two most important factors in determining satisfaction were good health and adequate financial resources. They reported finding other ways to satisfy their need to feel useful and to have a sense of responsibility. Almost half participated in volunteer work and about 40 percent found part-time work.

Retirement itself is a fairly recent notion. In 1900, the average American male spent about 3 percent of his lifetime in retirement. By 1980, the average retirement span had increased to about 10 percent.

Why work? Work can meet a variety of needs. It can:
- Give pattern to daily lives
- Provide status
- Improve how you feel about yourself
- Introduce you to new people
- Stimulate you intellectually
- Keep you active physically
- Help you feel useful and productive
- Give you a feeling of accomplishment

There are several ways to stay in the workforce, including working part-time, purchasing and operating a franchise, operating a small business, or beginning an entirely new career.

Retirees frequently choose to start new careers or open their own business in their new communities. Because of the state's rapid growth, a well-planned, -organized and -run business has a good chance to meet with success.

Job counselors recommend that you devise a timeline for making the transition to another job or business and then write an action plan. They also recommend brushing up on your job search skills, such as interviewing, researching, and negotiating.

Analysts say that most of Arizona's new jobs can be found in the service, retail, and manufacturing industries. In Arizona most new job growth has centered around the Phoenix and Tucson metropolitan areas. According to Arizona Department of Security economists, Phoenix nets about 75 percent of the new jobs and Tucson 19 percent, with the remaining jobs spread throughout the state.

Establishing a Business

Establishing a business in the state of Arizona is a relatively simple process. The fact-filled booklet, *Guide to Establishing a Business in Arizona*, is available from the Arizona Department of Commerce. In it you will find information about legal forms of business organization, registering a business, trademark and trade name laws, licensing requirements, taxation, environmental regulations, labor regulations, sources of funds, foreign trade zones, as well as a checklist for going into business.

Two useful publications for anyone considering locating a business in the state include *Arizona Community Profiles* and *Arizona County Profiles*. Check for prices by calling the Department of Commerce. To obtain either contact:

> Arizona Department of Commerce
> 3800 N. Central Ave. #1500
> Phoenix, AZ 85012
> 280-1321

Other valuable resources include the local Chamber of Commerce office in the community where you plan to live, networking groups, leads clubs, and fraternal, civic and social organizations. One of the keys to getting people to use your business is letting them know that you are there and want to be an active participant in the community.

Finding Work

If you are seeking more traditional employment, *Moving to Arizona*, can provide lists of employers as well as licensing, certification and registration requirements. You'll also find addresses for professional and trade organizations.

The Arizona Department of Economic Security publishes a variety of labor market publications.

Arizona Department of Economic Security
Labor Market Information
Publications
P.O. Box 6123
Phoenix, AZ 85005

Special Employment Needs

The Center for New Directions is a non-profit, community-based organization designed to help women over 35 re-enter the workforce. Call 252-0918 in Phoenix, 844-0187 in Mesa and 435-8530 in Glendale.

A number of organizations participate in the federal Jobs Training Partnership Act, some of which specialize in helping workers over 55.

Assistance for unemployed or underemployed Phoenix residents over 55 and seeking full or part-time work is available through the Older Workers Program sponsored by the City of Phoenix, Aging Services Division. Call 262-1876.

The Plus 50 Placement Center finds employment for needy applicants over 50 years of age and helps workers adapt skills to the marketplace. It is funded by United Way and the Department of Economic Security. For more information, call: 246-0260.

In Tucson, the Senior Resource Network is a non-profit community development source of information for anyone over 55. They supply information and refer individuals to other organizations. For more information, call: 795-7480.

8

Community Resources

Organizations, agencies and civic groups throughout the state have programs and activities designed to assist retirees. Many of these organizations serve as referral centers.

One agency you should know about is the Area Agency on Aging which coordinates the planning, development and delivery of services for persons over 60 years of age. The AAA coordinates advocacy efforts, promotes public awareness, and acts as an information center regarding programs and services for the aging.

In Maricopa County, the AAA office is located at:

1366 E. Thomas Rd. #108
Phoenix, AZ 85014
264-2255

This agency publishes an inexpensive, comprehensive directory of community resources. Contact the office directly for current price information.

In Pima County, the AAA is located at:
  5055 E. Broadway Blvd., Suite C104
  Tucson, AZ 85711
  790-7262
Other regional offices are located in Flagstaff, Yuma, Florence, Bisbee, Window Rock and at the Inter Tribal Council in Phoenix.

Referrals

Community Information & Referral is a free community service in both Phoenix and Tucson. A telephone helpline offers assistance in finding the appropriate human services. The Phoenix Community Information & Referral Services publishes a comprehensive annual *Human Services Directory,* which is more than 400 pages long and is used primarily by social service professionals. You can use your local library's copy or order direct. Check first for current prices.

  Community Information & Referral
  1515 E. Osborn Rd.
  Phoenix, AZ 85014
  263-8856

  Community Information & Referral
  2555 E. First St. #107
  Tucson, AZ 85716
  881-1794

For information about United Way agencies in Tucson contact:

  United Way
  6840 E. Broadway
  Tucson, AZ 85710
  722-6000

Volunteers

The Volunteer Centers in Phoenix, Mesa and Tucson recruit and refer volunteers for other non-profit agencies. Anyone from teens to senior citizens, including individuals or groups, can volunteer. The Maricopa County office publishes a free annual directory of agencies seeking volunteers. It provides basic information that can help in choosing the type of service in which you are most interested and for which you are qualified. The Tucson office has a column which appears in the Sunday paper listing volunteer needs.

For more information:

Volunteer Center
1515 E. Osborn Rd.
Phoenix, AZ 85014
263-9736

Volunteer Center
525 W. Southern Ave. #5
Mesa, AZ 85202
461-3198

Volunteer Center
6840 E. Broadway
Tucson, AZ 85710
886-6500

Appendix A

Community Profiles

On the following pages you'll find detailed information about communities that are home to many of the state's retirees. There's a place to suit everyone's tastes from small villages to major metropolitan areas. It's impossible to provide details on every potential retirement location, but this will get you pointed in the right direction. In addition to the communities profiled here, an address list for others is included. Peruse the following pages and select the locations that you want to visit. The difference between communities and commercially developed retirement communities is rather hazy. What may have started out as a commercial development may now be a community in its own right. It's next to impossible to keep up with the changes in the commercial developments. Where they are significant, we have mentioned them within the community's listings.

Phoenix and the Valley of the Sun

Apache Junction

Population: 18,365
County: Pinal
Location: 40 mi. e. of Phoenix
Elevation: 1,715
Rainfall: 7.52"
Snowfall: None

Average Temperatures:	Jan.	July
High	64.9	104.3
Low	35.6	74.1

Property Tax Rate Per $100 Assessed Valuation: $17.01

A popular haven for both retirees and snowbirds, Apache Junction is nestled near the base of the scenic Superstition Mountains where, as legend has it, the Lost Dutchman Mine is located. The Apache Trail meanders north out of the city past Canyon Lake, Apache Lake, and Lake Roosevelt.

Apache Junction's economy is based almost exclusively on recreation and retirement. The community is close to the resources of the big city, but just beyond the hustle and bustle. Mobile home living is a popular choice. RV living is popular among snowbirds. Valley Lutheran Hospital is just six miles to the west, and several other hospitals are nearby in Tempe, Mesa, and Phoenix. While a bit rustic, Apache Junction offers affordable housing for the budget-conscious.

For more information, contact:

Apache Junction Chamber of Commerce
P.O. Box 1747
Apache Junction, AZ 85217
982-3141

Avondale/ Goodyear/Litchfield Park

Population:
    Avondale: 20,410
    Goodyear: 6,465
    Litchfield Park: 3,360
County: Maricopa
Location: 15 mi. w. of Phoenix
Elevation: 1,017
Rainfall: 7.56"
Snowfall: None

Average Temperatures:	Jan.	July
High	66.9	106.8
Low	35.8	75.3

Property Tax Rate Per $100 Assessed Valuation:
    Avondale: $12.56
    Goodyear: $14.09
    Litchfield Park: $10.84

In 1916, the Goodyear Tire & Rubber Company purchased and leased land in the Salt River Valley to produce the strong Egyptian cotton used in making tire cords. The communities of Avondale, Goodyear and Litchfield Park were developed by the giant tire maker.

Avondale, the oldest of the three communities, was once a stage stop along the Phoenix to California wagon road. It's now situated in the midst of a bustling agricultural and industrial area of Maricopa County. The city was incorporated in 1946, although the post office was established 45 years earlier.

Goodyear, which was first called Egypt, but later renamed, was incorporated in the same year. In recent years, aerospace industries have broadened the employment base and today it encompasses 135 square miles. The Phoenix-Goodyear Airport has an 8,500 foot runway, one of the longest in the state. The community, while still rural, is poised for growth in the coming years.

Litchfield Park is the more upscale of these communities. Although settled in 1916, the town was incorporated in 1987 and has seen a flurry of development in the last few years. It's evolving into a planned community with emphasis on self-sufficient villages having their own stores, post offices, businesses and recreational facilities. The WigWam Resort is located here and Luke Air Force Base is nearby.

The desert and nearby Sierra Estrella and White Tank Mountains offer scenic views, hiking, rock hounding and horseback riding opportunities. Interstate 10 between Los Angeles and Phoenix passes through Goodyear providing easy access to the metro area. The nearest hospital is 12 miles away in Phoenix. A 24-hour emergency clinic is nearby.

For more information, contact:

Tri-City West Chamber of Commerce
501 W. Van Buren St.
Avondale, AZ 85323
932-2260

Carefree/Cave Creek

Population: 5,715
County: Maricopa
Location: 15 mi. ne. of Phoenix
Elevation: 2,500
Rainfall: 12.35"
Snowfall: .3"

Average Temperatures:	Jan.	July
High	62.0	102.0
Low	38.8	75.4

Property Tax Rate Per $100 Assessed Valuation: $8.29

Perched 1400 feet above the metro area, temperatures are usually a bit cooler here than on the desert's floor. Naturally-occurring piles of granite boulders mounded against the desert foothills offer striking views. Nearby, resorts and plush homes encircle designer golf courses. Deer, bobcat, coyotes, javelina, quail and even mountain lion still roam the area. The communities are the gateway to the Bartlett Lake recreation area.

Cave Creek was settled during the gold rush days of the early 1870s, but not incorporated until 1986. Neighboring Carefree, is the new kid on the block, founded in 1957. The developers were striving for a plush but village-like planned community that would blend with the desert. Strict architectural control has been a constant in the town's development. A 24-hour medical center handles local health needs. Complete hospital service is available in Phoenix and Scottsdale.

For more information, contact:

Carefree/Cave Creek Chamber of Commerce
P.O. Box 734
Carefree, AZ 85377
488-3381

Chandler

Population: 95,570
County: Maricopa
Location: 20 mi. se. of Phoenix
Elevation: 1,210
Rainfall: 8.42"
Snowfall: Trace

Average Temperatures:	Jan.	July
High	65.0	103.8
Low	37.3	76.4

Property Tax Rate Per $100 Assessed Valuation: $11.58

Chandler grew rapidly during the 1980s, due in part to high technology industries locating facilities in the area. The community was founded in 1911 by veterinarian and irrigation expert Dr. John Chandler, who also built Arizona's first exclusive resort hotel here in 1912. Today, downtown redevelopment revolves around the well-known San Marcos Hotel.

Until the recent wave of new arrivals discovered Chandler, the community was an agricultural trade center for ranchers, manufacturers, and processors. Chandler's Compadre Stadium is the winter home of the Milwaukee Brewers. Retirees who prefer to be near people of all ages will discover many young families in Chandler. A 160-bed hospital serves the community. Williams Air Force Base is nearby. Sun Lakes, a major retirement community with 8,000 residents is south of Chandler and east of Interstate 10.

For more information, contact:
> Chandler Chamber of Commerce
> 218 N. Arizona Ave.
> Chandler, AZ 85224
> 963-4571

Fountain Hills

Population: 10,475
County: Maricopa
Location: 30 mi. e. of Phoenix
Elevation: 1,500-3,300
Rainfall: 8.06"
Snowfall: None

Average Temperatures:

	Jan.	July
High	66.7	105.1
Low	36.4	74.2

Property Tax Per $100 Assessed Valuation: $10.92

Fountain Hills is an upscale, though casual, planned community with a population projection of 45,000. The development boasts of streets which deliberately curve to provide spectacular views stretching for miles, including glimpses of Red Rock, the Superstitions, Four Peaks and the McDowells.

Home prices range from $85,000 to more than $1 million. The community has its own churches, schools, service and social clubs, as well as medical and professional services. Mayo Clinic is a mile away and the nearest hospital is in Scottsdale. Golf, tennis, and other recreational facilities are nearby. Saguaro Lake is just 12 miles down the road. The McDowell Mountain range to the west separates the community from Scottsdale. Rio Verde is a smaller retirement community with about 600 homes located 10 minutes north of Fountain Hills.

For more information, contact:
> Fountain Hills Chamber of Commerce
> P.O. Box 17598
> Fountain Hills, AZ 85268
> 837-1654

Gilbert

Population: 33,385
County: Maricopa
Location: 15 mi. se. of Phoenix
Elevation: 1,273
Rainfall: 7.56"
Snowfall: Trace

Average Temperatures:	Jan.	July
High	64.9	104.3
Low	35.6	74.1

Property Tax Rate Per $100 Assessed Valuation: $13.16

Although one of the fastest growing towns in the United States, Gilbert still maintains the flavor and charm of the Old West. Country auctions, livestock shows, cattle ropings, potluck dinners and barbecues are a part of the everyday social scene.

One of the ten largest U.S. rodeos takes place here each November. Gilbert's population is expected to triple in the next ten years. Six hospitals in nearby Chandler and Mesa serve the community. Williams Air Force Base is nearby. Retirees report that Gilbert is "very peaceful."

For more information contact:

> Gilbert Chamber of Commerce
> P. O. Box 527
> Gilbert, AZ 85234
> 892-0056

Glendale

Population: 151,635
County: Maricopa
Location: W. of Phoenix
Elevation: 1,100
Rainfall: 6.74"
Snowfall: Trace

Average Temperatures:	Jan.	July
High	64.6	104.4
Low	38.0	78.3

Property Tax Rate Per $100 Assessed Valuation: $13.87

Founded in 1892 as a temperance colony by members of the fundamentalist Church of the Brethren, Glendale is still one of the largest fresh garden vegetable shipping points in the entire United States. Lettuce, broccoli, wheat, grapefruit, grapes, and cotton grow nearby. The city's population has tripled in the past 15 years. It is now the state's fifth largest city.

Luke Air Force Base, the nation's largest jet fighter training base, is just west of Glendale. Once primarily a blue collar bedroom community with strong agrarian ties, Glendale is now considered progressive, with a diverse population. The community is also the home of the American Graduate School of International Management (Thunderbird), known world-wide as a training institute for students of international business, and site of the annual Thunderbird Invitational Balloon Race. Saguaro Ranch is the center of many community activities, combining modern facilities with an historic farm. Three hospitals serve the community.

For more information contact:

        Glendale Chamber of Commerce
        P.O. Box 249
        Glendale, AZ 85311
        937-4754

Mesa

Population: 295,680
County: Maricopa
Location: 12 mi. e. of Phoenix
Elevation: 1,225
Rainfall: 7.52"
Snowfall: None

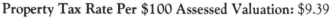

Average Temperatures:	Jan.	July
High	64.9	104.3
Low	35.6	74.1

Property Tax Rate Per $100 Assessed Valuation: $9.39

Mesa, the third largest city in the state and one of the fastest growing in the United States, was founded in 1878 by Mormons migrating from Utah. The city's name is from the bluff above the Salt River where the first settlers lived. The word "mesa" is Spanish for plateau. Mesa has grown into a diversified family-oriented community with a wide range of employment and retirement options. Between 1961 and 1988 Mesa's population grew by more than 500 percent.

Situated on the eastern edge of the metropolitan Phoenix area, Mesa forms the gateway to the majestic Superstition Mountains, rich in both Indian lore and gold mining mysteries.

Sirrine House and Crismon Farm and Heritage Museum preserve Mesa's pioneer history. Exhibits at the Mesa Southwest Museum trace the history of the Salt River Valley from pre-historic times to the present. HoHoKam Park is the winter home of the Chicago Cubs while the California Angels winter at Gene Autry Park. Four hospitals, 40 public parks, and no city property tax have enticed many newcomers to this East Valley location. Two large regional shopping malls are located here. Fountain of the Sun, Sunland Village, Sunland Village East, Dreamland and Leisure World are retirement developments located in Mesa, some of which no longer build new homes, but you may find resale homes there.

For more information, contact:
Mesa Chamber of Commerce
P.O. Box 5820
Mesa, AZ 85211
969-1307

Greater Paradise Valley

Population: 162,680
County: Maricopa
Location: Ne. Valley Metro Phoenix
Elevation: 1,421
Rainfall: 8.40"
Snowfall: Trace

Average Temperatures:	Jan.	July
High	64.5	104.1
Low	42.6	80.9

Property Tax Rate Per $100 Assessed Valuation: $11.03 (*Town of Paradise Valley*)

Greater Paradise Valley is located in a desert valley that extends over an area without precise boundaries, encompassing parts of the Town of Paradise Valley, Scottsdale and unincorporated areas of Maricopa County. In general, it is located north of MacDonald Drive, and south of Beardsley Road with borders at 7th Street to the west and Scottsdale Road to the east.

The Town of Paradise Valley, is a 14-square mile enclave within this area. Known for its predominantly large, expensive homes, the minimum lot size is one acre and all houses must be larger than 2,000 square feet. Asking price for the most inexpensive lot is a mere $150,000 and some mountainside lots command ten times that figure.

The town was incorporated in 1961, however, the community still clings to its rural lifestyle. There is no town property tax. Private firms handle many services normally provided by municipalities, such as trash removal, fire protection and water service, although Paradise Valley does have its own police department. Several hospitals serve the area.

For more information about the Greater Paradise Valley area or the Town of Paradise Valley, contact:

> Greater Paradise Valley Chamber of Commerce
> 3135 E. Cactus Rd.
> Phoenix, AZ 85032
> 482-3344

Peoria

Population: 53,505
County: Maricopa
Location: 11 mi. nw. of Phoenix
Elevation: 1,135
Rainfall: 7.65"
Snowfall: None

Average Temperatures:	Jan.	July
High	66.5	106.3
Low	35.0	74.7

Property Tax Rate Per $100 Assessed Valuation: $13.62

If the name sounds familiar, it may be because this westside community was settled in 1886 by four families from Peoria, Illinois who named the new community in honor of their midwestern home. Both communities share a rich agricultural heritage. Fields of cotton, citrus, vegetables, and fruit substitute for the wheat, corn and beans found in fertile central Illinois.

The city's northwest sector has been the focus of recent growth. It's a popular area for retirees, with Sun City on its western boundary. Luke Air Force Base, the world's largest jet fighter training facility, is to the southwest. Lake Pleasant Regional Park is just 15 miles away, offering varied water-based activities. There are five hospitals within a five mile radius. Westbrook Village, a retirement community with more than 3,000 residents is located north of Union Hills Drive near 91st Avenue.

For more information contact:
>   Peoria Chamber of Commerce
>   P.O. Box 70
>   Peoria, AZ 85380
>   979-3601

Phoenix

Population: 1,004,695
County: Maricopa
Location: 111 mi. n. of Tucson
Elevation: 1,135
Rainfall: 7.11"
Snowfall: None

Average Temperatures:	Jan.	July
High	64.6	104.4
Low	38.0	78.3

Property Tax Rate Per $100 Assessed Valuation: $12.05
(Average, varies by school district.)

Papago Park in Phoenix

Named for the mythical Phoenix bird which was consumed by fire every 500 years and rose anew from its own ashes, Phoenix was built on the ruins of the ancient Hohokam civilization. Phoenix's irrigation system today follows the canals designed by those early residents nearly 2,000 years ago.

Beginning as a small settlement on the Salt River banks in the mid 1860s, Phoenix spread outward in all directions until the city filled the Salt River Valley from north to south, spilling over into adjoining basins and overflowing into the suburban areas. Phoenix's growth spurt began after World War II when soldiers trained at the state's military centers returned here to live.

The city's crown jewels are encased within a 25,000-acre mountain preserve system, which provides breath-taking views and recreational opportunities the likes of which are not found in any other major U.S. city. In the past few years Phoenix has undertaken a major downtown redevelopment program.

Improved funding for the arts has dramatically improved facilities and cultural events. In 1989, Phoenix was selected as an All-American City. The Oakland A's hold spring training camp at Phoenix Stadium. Total medical care is available.

For more information, contact:

Phoenix Metropolitan Chamber of Commerce
34 W. Monroe St., Suite 900
Phoenix, AZ 85003
254-5521

Scottsdale

Population: 135,275
County: Maricopa
Location: E. of Phoenix
Elevation: 1,260
Rainfall: 7.05"
Snowfall: None

Average Temperatures:	Jan.	July
High	64.8	104.8
Low	37.6	77.5

Property Tax Rate Per $100 Assessed Valuation: $9.16

A city of contrasts, Scottsdale is a cowboy town, arts center, and resort playground. It was founded in 1888 by Army Chaplain Winfield Scott and incorporated in 1951 with less than one square mile. Today, the city is the one of the largest in the state, straddling the Valley from north to south.

Scottsdale's strict adherence to zoning gets much of the credit for the city's tidy appearance. In the "West's most western town," you can still hitch up your horse in the Old Town section or sit back and watch the world's largest horse-drawn parade wind through the streets each January. The city is a mecca for golfers and horse lovers alike, both of whom flock to the city to play in the sun. Nearly 100 galleries feature art ranging from the works of the Cowboy Artists of America to contemporary paintings and sculpture. The Indian Bend Greenbelt is a 7.5 mile flood control project in the heart of the city with parks, lakes and golf courses. Scottsdale is the winter home of the San Francisco Giants. Horseworld Park is the largest equestrian exhibition center in the U.S.

For more information contact:

Scottsdale Chamber of Commerce
P.O. Box 130
Scottsdale, AZ 85251
945-8481

Sun City/ Sun City West/ Surprise/ Youngtown
Population:
  Sun City: 38,455
  Sun City West: 17,293
  Surprise: 7,370
  Youngtown: 2,560
County: Maricopa
Location: 14-16 mi. nw. of Phoenix
Elevation: 1,117
Rainfall: 7.65"
Snowfall: None

Average Temperatures:	Jan.	July
High	64.8	104.8
Low	37.6	77.5

Property Tax Rate Per $100 Assessed Valuation:
  Sun City: $4.58
  Sun City West: $5.72
  Surprise: $15.61
  Youngtown: $4.83

Sun City is an 8,900 acre master-planned adult community northwest of Phoenix which opened in January, 1960. More than 100,000 visitors viewed the new community during its premiere, with 263 homes sold the first weekend. By the end of the year, Sun City was a community of 1,300 homes with a population of 2,500. More than 30 years later, with all residential property developed, Sun City's population is more than 42,000, making it the largest adult community in the United States.

Sun City West, a 5,705-acre development, will include just over 13,000 housing units and have a population of about 32,000 when completed. Like Sun City, Sun City West is a complete environment tailored to the needs and desires of persons 55 years or older. Both communities include recreational complexes, shopping centers, golf courses and medical facilities. The Sun Cities are known as a hub of activity with hundreds of civic, service, church, charitable and recreational clubs and organizations based in the communities. The communities are known for community pride, volunteer networks and low crime rates, as well as their active lifestyle. The Sundome Center for the Performing Arts is a stopping point for many big name entertainers. A Vacation program allows visitors to sample Sun Cities at reduced rates. For more information, phone (800) 528-2604.

Because of the Sun Cities' popularity as a retirement location, other retirement developments have clustered nearby. Two large RV parks in nearby Surprise host 5,000 winter visitors each year. Youngtown, America's oldest retirement community, is a quiet economical small town. Of the Sun Cities, new homes are available only in Sun City West, however, many resale homes are available in Sun City. Prices tend to be a bit higher for new homes. Lake Pleasant Regional Park and the White Tank Mountain Regional Park are a short drive away.

For more information, contact:
>   Northwest Valley Chamber of Commerce
>   12211 W. Bell Rd. Ste. 204
>   Surprise, AZ 85374
>   583-0692

>   Del Webb Corporation
>   13323 Meeker Blvd.
>   Sun City West, AZ 85375
>   974-7011

Tempe

Population: 144,115
County: Maricopa
Location: E. of Phoenix
Elevation: 1,105
Rainfall: 7.63"
Snowfall: None

Average Temperatures:	Jan.	July
High	65.5	104.3
Low	35.4	73.4

Property Tax Rate Per $100 Assessed Valuation: $11.87

Tempe bridges the dynamic growth occurring in Phoenix Metro's East and West valleys. As the home of Arizona State University and the site of the annual Fiesta Bowl, education and its related activities are a vital business in this community. Seventy-two percent of Tempe's residents are college educated. ASU Sun Devil Stadium is the scene of NFL action when the Phoenix Cardinals take to the fields.

Charles Trumbull Hayden arrived by wagon in 1873 and opened a mercantile store and flour mill. The Hayden Flour Mills are still in operation on the oldest continuously-used industrial site in the state. Preservationists have restored a 30-block area near ASU to the original territorial style. Twice a

year the Old Town area hosts the Festival of the Arts, one of
the 10 premier arts and crafts festivals in the United States.
Because of its location near the university many cultural and
sporting events take place in Tempe. The Seattle Mariners
train at Tempe Diablo Stadium. Older homes are clustered
near the university, while south Tempe is more upscale. Two
hospitals serve the community.

For more information contact:

> Tempe Chamber of Commerce
> 60 E. Fifth St.#3
> Tempe, AZ 85281
> 967-7891

Wickenburg

Population: 4,635
County: Maricopa
Location: 54 mi. nw. of Phoenix
Elevation: 2,100
Rainfall: 10.77"
Snowfall: Trace

Average Temperatures:	Jan.	July
High	63.3	103.6
Low	30.0	69.7

Property Tax Rate Per $100 Assessed Valuation: $10.40

The rolling foothills of the Bradshaw Mountains along the
banks of the Hassayampa River, gold mines and ghost towns
beckon retirees to Wickenburg. Prussian native Henry
Wickenburg arrived in Arizona in 1862 and discovered the
Vulture Mine. Gold miners prospected the area until 1909
when the deposits were exhausted. Those who remained
turned to farming and cattle ranching.

Today more than two-thirds of residents earn their living
servicing the tourism industry. The ghost towns of Stanton,
Congress, Weaverville and abandoned gold mines like the Abe

Lincoln, Monte Cristo, and Vulture are nearby. Naturalists are attracted to Saguaro Forest, Joshua Tree Forest, and Ocotillo Flat. The Desert Caballeros Museum has one of the state's best collections of western bronzes. Lake Pleasant Regional Park is nearby. A small hospital and several physicians provide for the community's health needs with consultation available from specialists in the Metro Phoenix area.

For more information, contact:
Wickenburg Chamber of Commerce
215 Frontier St.
Wickenburg, AZ 85358
684-5479

Southern Arizona

Arizona City
Population: 2,002
County: Pinal
Location: 56 mi. se. of Phoenix
Elevation: 1,505
Rainfall: 8.45"
Snowfall: Trace

Average Temperatures:	Jan.	July
High	67.0	105.0
Low	35.7	75.1

Property Tax Rate Per $100 Assessed Valuation: $19.11

Arizona City, a planned community located almost exactly between Tucson and Phoenix in the Santa Cruz Basin, offers residents easy access to both metropolitan areas, yet a peaceful small-town lifestyle.

Situated in the heart of one of the state's most productive agricultural areas, local farms produce cotton, jojoba beans, grains, vegetables, and citrus. There's an 18-hole championship golf course for the duffer and a 48-acre lake for sailing and fishing. Rock hounds will love the Agate Fields just south of Arizona City. The state's only Civil War battle took place at Picacho Peak, just 22 miles southeast, where troops from the Union's California Volunteers encountered the Confederacy's Texas Volunteers. Complete medical facilities are available in Casa Grande, 20 miles to the north.

For more information, contact:
Arizona City Chamber of Commerce
Box 5
Arizona City, AZ 85223
466-5141

Casa Grande
Population: 19,415
County: Pinal
Location: 45 mi. se. of Phoenix
Elevation: 1,398
Rainfall: 8.12"
Snowfall: Trace

Average Temperatures:	Jan.	July
High	66.0	106.2
Low	35.0	76.0

Property Tax Rate Per $100 Assessed Valuation: $14.96

Casa Grande is strategically located in the "central corridor" between Phoenix and Tucson, just six miles from the intersection of Interstates 8 and 10.

Until recently, the area was predominantly agrarian, but manufacturing, retail, government, and tourist-related industries now account for a much larger share of the workforce. A 100-bed hospital serves the community.

Founded in 1879, the town was named for the famous Casa Grande Indian ruins located 20 miles to the northeast in Coolidge. At the Casa Grande Ruins visitors can view well-preserved remains of a central four-story building and several

smaller outlying buildings constructed by the Hohokam
Indians during the 13th century. The Gila River and the
Tohono O'odham Indian reservations are nearby.

For more information, contact:

> Greater Casa Grande Chamber of Commerce
> 575 N. Marshall
> Casa Grande, AZ 85222
> 836-2125

Florence

Population: 7,750
County: Pinal
Location: 61 mi. se. of Phoenix
Elevation: 1,493
Rainfall: 9.50"
Snowfall: None

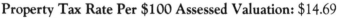

Average Temperatures:	Jan.	July
High	66.8	106.1
Low	36.1	74.0

Property Tax Rate Per $100 Assessed Valuation: $14.69

Just beyond the metro Phoenix area, Arizona retirees have
discovered Florence in the midst of a region dominated by an
agricultural-based economy. Cotton, cattle, sugar beets, grains,
and grapes are staple products. A third of the workforce is
involved in public administration. Nine hundred employees
staff the Arizona State Prison.

Florence was settled in 1866 and named by Governor
Richard McCormick in 1868. Levi Ruggles, an Indian agent,
was the first settler. Many of the community's buildings are
listed on the National Register of Historic Places. McFarland
State Park is located in the county's first courthouse, which
has been restored to its original 1880s condition. At nearby
Poston Butte, you'll find a monument marking the grave of
Charles D. Poston, who is known as the "Father of Arizona."

It's a 45-minute drive to Phoenix or to Tucson from Florence. The community has a hospital and 45 physicians who service the area's health needs.

For more information, contact:
Florence Chamber of Commerce
P.O. Box 929
Florence, AZ 85232
868-9443

Green Valley

Population: 21,087
County: Pima
Location: 25 mi. s. of Tucson
Elevation: 2,900
Rainfall: 10.86"
Snow: 1"

Average Temperatures:	Jan.	July
High	67.1	101.3
Low	31.0	68.4

Property Tax Rate Per $100 Assessed Valuation: $10.69

Green Valley is nestled midway between Tucson and Nogales in the fertile Santa Cruz River Valley. This adult retirement community was established in 1964.

Occupying part of the vast San Ignacio De las Canoa Grant, the territory was given to "New Spain" by the Spanish crown in the 16th century. Early Spanish missions, frontier outposts, and old mines pepper the area around Green Valley. The Historic San Xavier del Bac Mission is 18 miles to the north and the Tumacacori National Monument 30 miles south. Both were Jesuit missions built in the early 1700s. Mount Hopkins Observatory, operated by the Smithsonian Institute, is 20 miles southeast of Green Valley. The Titan Missile Museum is located in Green Valley. Nearby Madera Canyon offers the best in bird watching.

Primarily a retirement community, Green Valley has nine recreational centers, six golf courses and 23 heated swimming pools. There is a 24-hour emergency clinic in Green Valley. The nearest hospital is in Tucson.

For more information, contact:

Green Valley Chamber of Commerce
P.O. Box 566
Green Valley, AZ 85622
625-7575

Pearce Sunsites

Population: 1,212
County: Cochise
Location: 85 mi. se. of Tucson
Elevation: 4,500
Rainfall: 11.57"
Snowfall: 1.2"

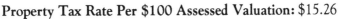

Average Temperatures:	Jan.	July
High	61.3	94.2
Low	29.4	64.3

Property Tax Rate Per $100 Assessed Valuation: $15.26

The rugged Dragoon Mountains and broad grassy valleys of Cochise County were once the domain of Apaches, Cochise and Geronimo. Today, retirees have taken to the moderate climate of the San Pedro Valley. Along the Cochise Trail near the gateway to Mexico, the Horizon Corporation began developing the master-planned retirement community in 1961. At 4,500 feet, the community has mild temperatures year-round.

Cochise County is largely agricultural and there is limited opportunity for employment in Arizona Sunsites. A community medical clinic serves the area, with the nearest hospitals at Willcox and Benson.

The mountain ranges surrounding the San Pedro Valley offer outdoor recreation and hunting. Cochise Stronghold, a camping and picnic ground maintained by the National Forest Service, is just eight miles from Pearce Sunsites. The Amerind Foundation, an archaeological research center and museum, is nearby.

For more information contact:
Pearce Sunsites Chamber of Commerce
P.O. Box 308
Pearce, AZ 85625
826-3535

Sierra Vista
Population: 33,275
County: Cochise
Location: 70 mi. se. of Tucson
Elevation: 4,625
Rainfall: 22.55"
Snowfall: 1"

Average Temperatures:	Jan.	July
High	58.4	88.6
Low	34.2	66.4

Property Tax Rate Per $100 Assessed Valuation: $14.59

Sierra Vista, from the Spanish for "mountain view," lies in the midst of the Whetstone, Dragoon, Mule, and Huachuca Mountains. Fort Huachuca was established in 1877 to protect pioneers from renegade Apaches.

Climatologists rank Sierra Vista as one of the most temperate regions in the nation, with an average maximum temperature of 75 degrees and an average minimum of 50 degrees. The city overlooks the San Pedro Valley and has one of the most diverse mammal populations in the world.

The community's largest employer is Fort Huachuca, but an increasing number of high technology industries are locating here. About 72 percent of Sierra Vista's heads of households have college educations. The Nature Conservancy at nearby Ramsey Canyon boasts the largest number of hummingbird species in the United States. Three hospitals serve the community.

For more information contact:

Sierra Vista Chamber of Commerce
77 Calle Portal #A140
Sierra Vista, AZ 85635
458-6940

Tubac

Population: 897
County: Santa Cruz
Location: 45 mi. s. of Tucson
Rainfall: 14.22"
Snowfall: .5"

Average Temperatures:	Jan.	July
High	65.9	97.1
Low	31.2	65.5

Property Tax Rate Per $100 Assessed Valuation: $11.30

Tubac is in the extreme southern part of Arizona about 40 miles north of the Mexican-U.S. border. It lies in a valley of the Santa Cruz River at the foot of the Santa Rita Mountain range. Originally settled by Indian farmers, the Spanish military established a "presidio" here in 1752, making it Arizona's oldest European settlement. From this base, Juan De Anza led an expedition to California and founded San Francisco. When the presidio was moved to Tucson in 1776, the Apaches regained the area.

Tourism and retirement play dominant roles in the community's economy. Two thirds of the population is retired or semi-retired. More than 125,000 visitors come here each year. Tubac has an international reputation as an artist colony with major art festivals held in February and November. Specialty shops display local arts and crafts. Tumcacori National Monument is nearby. The nearest hospital is in Nogales, 23 miles away.

For more information, contact:

Tubac Chamber of Commerce
P.O. Box 1866
Tubac, AZ 85646
398-2704

Tucson

Population: 415,788
County: Pima
Location: 111 mi. s. of Phoenix
Elevation: 2,584
Rainfall: 11.05"
Snowfall: .6"

Average Temperatures:	Jan.	July
High	66.0	101.1
Low	36.7	73.3

Property Tax Rate Per $100 Assessed Valuation: $14.02

From a lookout on Sentinel Peak the expansive Tucson Valley can be seen. Mountain ranges encircle the Valley which is created by the majestic Santa Catalina Mountains on the north and northeast, the Rincon Mountains on the east, the Santa Rita and Sierrita Mountains on the south and southeast, the Tucson Mountains on the west and the Tortolita Mountains to the northwest. The Santa Cruz River, Rillito River, and Pantano Wash waterways cut through the city.

Jesuit missionary Father Eusibio Francisco Kino explored the area in 1687. At that time the land was occupied by Pima and Sbaipuri Indians. A community was established in 1775 by
marginhelper

Tucson is flanked by mountains.

Spanish soldiers for the Presidente de San Augustave Del Tucson. Today, Tucson is still the "Old Pueblo." Excavations have revealed evidence of prehistoric civilizations dating to the ninth century.

Tucson's Spanish, Mexican, Indian and pioneer influences have endured. Indian arts and crafts, pioneer homes as well as Mexican food and architecture are deeply ingrained in the culture.

Federal, state and local government employ 50,000. The University of Arizona and Davis-Monthan Air Force Base are major employers. High technology and tourism also play major roles in the city's economy. Business, industry, sports and culture combine with the desert beauty. The Arizona-Sonoran Desert Museum and Old Tucson movie town are major attractions. The Cleveland Indians hold spring training camp at Hi Corbett Field. Complete medical facilities are available, including a major research hospital. Sun City Tucson is located 10 miles northwest. Saddlebrooke is another Tucson retirement development.

For more information, contact:

> Tucson Metropolitan Chamber of Commerce
> P.O. Box 991
> Tucson, AZ 85702
> 792-2250

Yuma

Population: 56,105
County: Yuma
Location: 184 mi. se. of Phoenix
Elevation: 138
Rainfall: 2.99"
Snowfall: None

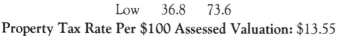

Average Temperatures:	Jan.	July
High	68.4	106.6
Low	36.8	73.6

Property Tax Rate Per $100 Assessed Valuation: $13.55

Originally known as Colorado City, then Arizona City, and even Yuma City, this community was finally reincorporated as Yuma in 1873, although settlers arrived twenty years earlier.

Located in the far southwestern corner of Arizona where the Gila and Colorado rivers meet, the city is surrounded by 192,000 acres of irrigated farms and feedlot cattle operations which send 99,000 animals to market each year.

As with many other Arizona communities, the military is an important influence. An Army proving ground and a Marine air station are here. Cross-country travelers and winter visitors pump $250 million into the local economy each year.

At just 138 feet above sea level, Yuma has the lowest elevation of any Arizona community. Yuma International Airport has daily commuter service to Phoenix and Los

Angeles. The San Diego Padres train at Desert Sun Stadium. The Old Territorial Prison and Fort Yuma are major tourist attractions. The Colorado River and the nearby California sand dunes provide other recreation. San Luis, Mexico, is just 25 miles to the south.

For more information, contact:

>Yuma County Chamber of Commerce
>P.O. Box 230
>Yuma, AZ 85366
>782-2567

Northern Arizona

Camp Verde

Population: 6,550
County: Yavapai
Location: 86 mi. n. Phoenix
Elevation: 3,133
Rainfall: 19.24"
Snowfall: 2.0"

Average Temperatures:	Jan.	July
High	56.5	107.1
Low	29.0	60.5

Property Tax Rate Per $100 Assessed Valuation: $13.95

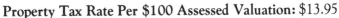

The Verde Valley's high desert location eliminates the summer sizzle found at lower elevations, yet is low enough to protect the area from the harsh winters at the upper elevations. The mild, dry, four-season climate attracts many retirees. Year-round temperatures average 80.6 for the high and 44.6 for the low.

Early Arizona settlers gathered at Camp Verde seeking protection from Indian raids. The military post moved from the river to higher ground in 1871. It once served as headquarters for General George Crook and his soldiers, scouts and pack mules. Today, that site is a state park which features military artifacts, Indian relics and articles used by the early settlers. Recently incorporated, Camp Verde now covers 48 square miles. The nearest hospital is 16 miles west at Cottonwood.

For more information contact:
Camp Verde Chamber of Commerce
P.O. Box 1665
Camp Verde, AZ 86322
567-9294

Cottonwood/Verde Valley
Population: 38,000
County: Yavapai
Location: 101 mi. n. of Phoenix
Elevation: 3,100-4,600
Rainfall: 12.21"
Snowfall: 5"

Average Temperatures:	Jan.	July
High	58.2	98.4
Low	28.4	66.0

Property Tax Rate Per $100 Assessed Valuation: $8.10-$10.70

The Verde Valley was named for the Verde River and the lush growth along its banks. The area encompasses the communities of Camp Verde, Clarkdale, Cottonwood, Jerome, Bridgeport and Cornville.

As the Verde Valley's trading center, Cottonwood offers a full range of retail and professional services. The Old Town area provides an atmosphere of an old, western downtown street with high sidewalks and false-fronted buildings. Nearly half of area residents are retired. Between 1980 and 1988 the Verde Valley grew by 23 percent.

A wealth of scenic, historic and recreational activities await visitors to the Verde Valley including: Tuzigoot National

Monument, Montezuma's Castle National Monument, Montezuma's Well and the ghost town of Jerome. Four state parks offer additional recreational activities. There is a hospital in Cottonwood.

For more information, contact:
>   Cottonwood/Verde Valley Chamber of Commerce
>   1010 S. Main St.
>   Cottonwood, AZ 86326
>   634-7593

Flagstaff

Population: 47,230
County: Coconino
Location: 146 mi. n. of Phoenix
Elevation: 7,000
Rainfall: 19.80"
Snowfall: 84.4"

Average Temperatures:	Jan.	July
High	42.2	81.9
Low	14.6	50.6

Property Tax Rate Per $100 Assessed Valuation: $ 9.88

In a state of contrasts, the cool climate, northern Arizona community of Flagstaff provides balance. At 7,000 feet elevation, the city receives over 80 inches of snow annually and summers are very mild.

The majestic San Francisco Peaks stretch over 12,643 feet. Lumber is harvested from the forests of the region. Lowell Observatory is a major astronomy research center. Hunters come in search of antelope, deer, elk, black bear, wildcat, turkey, and small game birds. Snow skiing is a popular winter sport.

From Flagstaff, it's a short drive to the Grand Canyon, Walnut Canyon, Sunset Crater, Oak Creek Canyon, Glen Canyon, and the Hopi and Navajo Indian reservations.

Flagstaff is the major tourist and trade center of northern Arizona. With 11,896,720 acres, Coconino County is the second largest county in the United States. Flagstaff became the county seat in 1891 and was incorporated three years later.

For more information, contact:

Flagstaff Chamber of Commerce
101 West Route 66
Flagstaff, AZ 86001
774-4505

Heber/Overgaard

Population: 5,600
County: Navajo
Location: 140 mi. ne. of Phoenix
Elevation: 6,250
Rainfall: 17.04"
Snowfall: 51.3"

Average Temperatures:	Jan.	July
High	46.1	84.7
Low	14.7	51.6

Property Tax Rate Per $100 Assessed Valuation: $8.94

In the midst of the Sitgreaves National Forest just a bit north of the Mogollon Rim are the communities of Heber and Overgaard. Tourism and retirement related businesses are important to these two communities. In summer the population doubles as city dwellers come searching for calm, cool surroundings.

Heber was established in 1876 by Mormon families and is named for Heber C. Kimbell, a prominent church member. Overgaard is a mile east of Heber. A. Dane Overgaard moved to the area in 1936 to establish a sawmill camp that grew into a larger community.

Hunting and fishing opportunities lure visitors to the area year-round. Within 50 miles there are 32 lakes and 400 miles of trout streams. The timber industry is the primary economic activity. There is a hospital at Show Low, 36 miles away.

For more information, contact:

> Heber/Overgaard Chamber of Commerce
> P.O. Box 550
> Heber, AZ 85928
> 535-4406

Lake Havasu City

Population: 27,685
County: Mohave
Location: 200 mi. nw. of Phoenix
Elevation: 482 feet
Rainfall: 3.82"
Snowfall: None

Average Temperatures:	Jan.	July
High	67.3	108.6
Low	37.1	78.8

Property Tax Rate Per $100 Assessed Valuation: $14.30

Founded in 1963, Lake Havasu City is a planned community for people of all ages. In 1989 it was a National Take Pride in America award winner. Located on the east banks of Lake Havasu, on the Colorado River, the city's population has grown at a rate of about 1,000 residents per year. The median age here is just over 34. Less than 12 percent of the population is over 65. The town was developed by McCullough Properties, Inc.

Las Vegas is 150 miles to the north and Los Angeles 350 miles to the west. It's a short trip to the casinos in nearby Laughlin, Nevada.

London Bridge at Lake Havasu City

The community is best known as the second home of the historic London Bridge. Opened in October 1971, the bridge was moved brick-by-brick from its London, England location to Lake Havasu City. The bridge and the surrounding English village are the focal point of a multi-million dollar resort complex of shops, restaurants, and lodging facilities.

Rockhounds will find volcanic rock, geodes, jaspers, obsidians, turquoise, and agate nearby. Fishing enthusiasts come for the striped and large mouth bass, bluegill, catfish and crappie. Skiing and boating are also popular activities.

For more information contact:

> Lake Havasu City Visitor and Convention Bureau
> 1930 Mesquite Ave. # 3
> Lake Havasu City, AZ 86403
> 855-4155

Parker

Population: 2,964
County: LaPaz
Location: 162 mi. w. of Phoenix
Elevation: 450
Rainfall: 3.82"
Snowfall: Trace

Average Temperatures:	Jan.	July
High	67.3	108.6
Low	37.1	78.8

Property Tax Rate Per $100 Assessed Valuation: $9.32

Parker was first settled in 1871, but began to prosper in 1938 when Parker Dam, the world's deepest dam was built to create Lake Havasu. The new dam brought water for irrigation and recreation. The 11-mile strip of the Colorado River between Parker Dam and Headgate Rock Dam form one of finest bodies of water in the country for water-based recreational activities. Bass, crappie, bluegill, catfish, trout fishing and frogging are popular. Agriculture is still an important economic influence. Melons, lettuce, cotton, wheat, barley and alfalfa are produced here. The 100,000-acre Colorado River Indian Reservation is nearby. Parker is the county seat for LaPaz County, the youngest of Arizona's counties which was formed in 1982, when it was separated from Yuma County. A 39-bed hospital serves the community.

For more information contact:
Parker Area Chamber of Commerce
P.O. Box 627
Parker, AZ 85344
669-2174

Payson

Population: 8,660
County: Gila
Location: 94 mi. ne. of Phoenix
Elevation: 5,000
Rainfall: 20.77"
Snowfall: 25.1"

Average Temperatures:	Jan.	July
High	53.1	92.5
Low	13.7	58.5

Property Tax Rate Per $100 Assessed Valuation: $12.34

First settled in 1881 as a gold mining camp, Payson was originally known as Union Park. Located in the exact center of Arizona and nestled among the world's largest stand of Ponderosa pine, Payson offers hunting, fishing, camping, and hiking. Hunting for elk, deer, turkey, antelope, bear, javelina, and mountain lion are permitted in season. Mountain trout streams and well-stocked lakes beckon the angler. Tonto Natural Bridge and the Zane Grey Cabin are local attractions. The Loggers and Sawdust Festival is held in late July and the annual Rodeo and Parade held each August is more than 100 years old.

Located just below the Mogollon Rim at an elevation of 5,000 feet, the city has been cited for its pure "ozone belt" which may contribute to good health. Retirees are attracted to the mild four-season climate of the area. There is a local 44-bed hospital.

For more information contact:

Payson Chamber of Commerce
P.O. Box 1380
Payson, AZ 85547
474-4515

Pine/Strawberry

Population: 3,905
County: Gila
Location: 110 mi. ne. of Phoenix
Elevation: Pine 5,440/Strawberry 6,047
Rainfall: 20.77"
Snowfall: 23.7"

Average Temperatures:	Jan.	July
High	53.1	92.5
Low	23.7	58.5

Property Tax Rate Per $100 Assessed Valuation: $11.84

With a combined population of just over 2,000 these two communities 15 miles north of Payson offer the seclusion, natural beauty and recreational activities that retirees longing to"get away from it all" will appreciate.

Pine takes its name from the pine forests surrounding the community. Strawberry was named for the abundant wild strawberries in the area. Both have mild four-season climates.

In the summer months, the population doubles as visitors come to refresh in the beautiful pine-clad country. Campgrounds are plentiful. Fishermen frequent Blue Ridge Reservoir, Bear Canyon Lake and Knoll Lake as well as 250 miles of nearby trout streams. Tourists and second-home residents contribute heavily to the local economy.

For more information, contact:
Pine/Strawberry Chamber of Commerce
Box 333
Pine, AZ 85544
476-3547

Prescott

Population: 27,050
County: Yavapai
Location: 96 mi. nw. of Phoenix
Elevation: 5,347
Rainfall: 18.10"
Snowfall: 23.7"

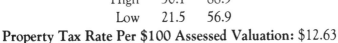

Average Temperatures: Jan.   July
              High   50.1   88.9
              Low   21.5   56.9

Property Tax Rate Per $100 Assessed Valuation: $12.63

Just west of the geographic center of Arizona on the slopes of the Bradshaw Mountains, Prescott has long attracted retirees seeking a temperate climate. About a quarter of the population is retired. The community has long been a haven for relief from respiratory ailments.

Town Square in Prescott

The town was established in 1864 after gold was discovered, and for a short time was Arizona's territorial capital. Prescott is rich in historic and scenic attractions, including museums, scenic drives, lakes, and annual events. At hand is the Prescott National Forest with more than a million acres, scenic Thumb Butte, Granite Dells, and Mingus Mountain. Historic Whiskey Row and the Sharlot Hall Museum shouldn't be missed.

A town square and charming frame homes contrast with the stucco and tile found in southern Arizona. Prescott is found on the list of choice locations of such publications as the *Wall Street Journal*, the *Chicago Tribune*, and *Newsweek*. There are two hospitals here including one veterans' hospital.

For more information contact:

Prescott Chamber of Commerce
P.O. Box 1147
Prescott, AZ 86302
445-2000

Sedona

Population: 14,250
County: Coconino
Location: 127 mi. n. of Phoenix
Elevation: 4,300
Rainfall: 17.15"
Snowfall: 8.8"

Average Temperatures:	Jan.	July
High	55.0	95.1
Low	29.7	65.1

Property Tax Rate Per $100 Assessed Valuation: $7.67

On Oak Creek Canyon's southern edge, Sedona attracts close to three million visitors each year. Residents include retailers, artists, writers, and craftsmen as well as retirees. More than 100 galleries and craft shops are located here.

The town takes its name from early settler, Sedona Schnebly, who was among those populating the area in 1902. The area is called Red Rock Country because of the spectacular red sandstone formations, or more accurately, monolithic formations of red Supai sandstone. Slide Rock State Park, and recently opened Red Rock State Park, provide additional public access to the scenic Sedona countryside.

For more information contact:

Sedona-Oak Creek Chamber of Commerce
P.O. Box 478
Sedona, AZ 86336
282-7722

Other Chamber of Commerce Offices

Ajo
321 Taladro
Ajo, AZ 85321
(602) 387-7742

Alpine
P .O. Box 410
Alpine, AZ 85920
(602) 339-4330

Bisbee
Drawer BA
Bisbee, AZ 85603
(602) 432-5421

Bullhead Area
P.O. Box 66
Bullhead City, AZ 86430
(602) 754-4121

Chino Valley
P.O. Box 419
Chino Valley, AZ 86322
(602) 636-2493

Coolidge
141 N. Main St.
Coolidge, AZ 85228
(602) 723-7647

Gila Bend
P.O. Box CC
Gila Bend, AZ 85337
(602) 683-2074

Globe-Miami
P.O. Box 2539
Globe, AZ 85502
(602) 425-4495

Holbrook
100 E. Arizona
Holbrook, AZ 86025
(602) 524-6558

Kingman Area
P.O. Box 1150
Kingman, AZ 86402
(602) 753-6106

Nogales-Santa Cruz
Kino Park
Nogales, AZ 85621
(602) 287-3685

Page-Lake Powell
P.O. Box 727
Page, AZ 86040

Quartzsite
P.O. Box 85
Quartzsite, AZ 85346
(602) 927-5600

Show Low
P.O. Box 1083
Show Low, AZ 85901
(602) 537-2326

Springerville/Eager
P.O. Box 181
Springerville, AZ 85938
(602) 333-2123

Tombstone
P.O. Box 995
Tombstone, AZ 85638
(602) 457-9317

Williams-Grand Canyon
820 W. Bill Williams Ave.
Williams, AZ 86046
(602) 635-4061

Appendix B

County Roundup

Apache

Location: Northeastern corner
Year Founded: 1879
County Seat: St. Johns
Major Cities: Eager, Fort Defiance, St. Johns, Chinle, Window Rock, Springerville
Square Miles: 11,212
Population: 62,550
Density: 6.2 Persons Per Square Mile
Major Industries: Lumber, tourism, cattle, government, utilities
Attractions: Petrified Forest National Park, Painted Desert, Canyon de Chelly, Four Corners, Window Rock, Big Lake, Hawley Lake, Lyman Lake State Park, Sunrise Ski Area

Cochise
Location: Southeastern corner
Year Founded: 1881
County Seat: Bisbee
Major Cities: Sierra Vista, Douglas, Bisbee, Willcox, Benson
Square Miles: 6,219
Population: 99,300
Density: 16.9 Persons Per Square Mile
Major Industries: Farming, ranching, tourism, military
Attractions: Chiricahua National Monument, Coronado National Monument, Tombstone, Bisbee, Fort Huachuca, Cochise Stronghold

Coconino (co-co-NEE-no)
Location: Northern border
Year Founded: 1891
County Seat: Flagstaff
Major Cities: Flagstaff, Sedona, Page, Tuba City, Williams
Square Miles: 18,608
Population: 99,150
Density: 5.2 Persons Per Square Mile
Major Industries: Tourism, recreation, forestry, ranching, government
Attractions: Grand Canyon National Park, Sunset Crater National Monument, Wupatki National Monument, Walnut Canyon National Monument, Oak Creek Canyon, Museum of Northern Arizona, Lowell Observatory, Meteor Canyon National Monument, San Francisco Peaks, Snow Bowl Ski Area, Riordan State Historic Park, Rim Lakes

Gila (HEE-luh)

Location: Central/eastern region
Year Founded: 1881
County Seat: Globe
Major Cities: Payson, Globe, Miami,
Square Miles: 4,752
Population: 40,550
Density: 9.0 Persons Per Square Mile
Major Industries: Copper mining, ranching, lumber, tourism, recreation
Attractions: Tonto National Monument, Salt River Canyon, Besh Ba Gowah, Roosevelt Lake, Zane Grey Cabin, Tonto Natural Bridge

Graham
Location: Near eastern border/southern region
Year Founded: 1881
County Seat: Safford
Major Cities: Safford, Thatcher, Pima
Square Miles: 4,630
Population: 27,050
Density: 5.7 Persons Per Square Mile
Major Industries: Farming, ranching, tourism, recreation
Attractions: Mt. Graham, San Carlos Lake, Aravaipa Canyon, Roper Lake State Park

Greenlee
Location: Along eastern border/southern region
Year Founded: 1909
County Seat: Clifton
Major Cities: Clifton, Duncan
Square Miles: 1,838
Population: 7,725
Density: 4.6 Persons Per Square Mile
Major Industries: Copper mining, ranching, tourism
Attractions: Coronado Trail, Hannagan Meadow, Blue River

La Paz
Location: Central western border
Year Founded: 1983
County Seat: Parker
Major Cities: Parker, Salome
Square Miles: 4,484
Population: 14,025
Density: 3.3 Persons Per Square Mile

Major Industries: agriculture, tourism, light manufacturing,
government
Attractions: Colorado River, Parker Dam, Colorado River Indian
Tribes Museum

Maricopa (MARE-i-CO-pah)
Location: Central/southern region
Year Founded: 1871
County Seat: Phoenix
Major Cities: Phoenix, Mesa, Tempe, Glendale, Scottsdale,
Chandler, Sun City, Peoria
Square Miles: 9,127
Population: 2,180,575
Density: 233.7 Persons Per Square Mile
Major Industries: High tech manufacturing, agriculture, tourism,
travel
Attractions: Heritage Square, Phoenix Art Museum, Heard
Museum, Arizona State Capitol Museum, Arizona Mineral Museum,
Desert Botanical Garden, Pueblo Grande Museum, Phoenix Zoo,
Desert Caballeros Museum

Mohave (moe-HAH-vee)
Location: Northwestern corner
Year Founded: 1864
County Seat: Kingman
Major Cities: Bullhead City, Lake Havasu City, Kingman
Square Miles: 13,286
Population: 98,900
Density: 6.8 Persons Per Square Mile
Major Industries: Manufacturing, tourism, ranching
Attractions: Grand Canyon National Park, London Bridge,

Navajo
Location: North and east near borders
Year Founded: 1895
County Seat: Holbrook
Major Cities: Winslow, Holbrook, Show Low, Kayenta, Snowflake
Square Miles: 9,955
Population: 78,725
Density: 8.6 Persons Per Square Mile
Major Industries: Tourism, coal mining, manufacturing, lumber, ranching
Attractions: Petrified Forest National Park, Painted Desert, Hopi Indian Villages, Navajo National Monument, Monument Valley, White Mountains

Pima
Location: Southern border/central
Year Founded: 1864
County Seat: Tucson
Major Cities: Tucson, Green Valley, South Tucson, Ajo, Marana
Square Miles: 9,188
Population: 682,075
Density: 75.3 Persons Per Square Mile
Major Industries: Copper mining, manufacturing, tourism, education
Attractions: Organ Pipe Cactus National Monument, Saguaro National Monument, Mt. Lemmon, Sabino Canyon, Arizona Sonoran Desert Museum, San Xavier del Bac Mission, Kitt Peak National Observatory, Colossal Cave, Old Tucson, Titan Missile Museum, Pima Air Museum

Pinal (pee-NAL)

Location: Central/southern region
Year Founded: 1875
County Seat: Florence
Major Cities: Casa Grande, Apache Junction, Coolidge, Eloy, Florence, Superior
Square Miles: 5,344
Population: 119,050
Density: 21.4 Persons Per Square Mile
Major Industries: Farming, ranching, copper mining, tourism, manufacturing
Attractions: Casa Grande Ruins National Monument, Superstition Mountains, Weaver's Needle, Picacho Peak State Park, Pinal Pioneer Parkway, McFarland State Historic Park, Boyce Thompson Southwestern Arboretum, Aravaipa Canyon Wilderness

Santa Cruz

Location: Southern border
Year Founded: 1899
County Seat: Nogales
Major Cities: Nogales, Patagonia
Square Miles: 1,238
Population: 30,950
Density: 24.1 Persons Per Square Mile
Major Industries: Tourism, international trade, manufacturing, services, government
Attractions: Nogales, Mexico, Tumacacori National Monument, Pena Blanca Lake, Tubac, Patagonia Lake

Yavapai (YA-vuh-pie)
Location: Central/northern region
Year Founded: 1864
County Seat: Prescott
Major Cities: Prescott, Prescott Valley, Cottonwood, Chino Valley, Bagdad
Square Miles: 8,122
Population: 111,975
Density: 18.1 Persons Per Square Mile
Major Industries: Tourism, recreation, ranching, manufacturing, copper mining
Attractions: Montezuma Castle National Monument, Montezuma's Well, Tuzigoot National Monument, Granite Dells, Joshua Forest Parkway, Sharlot Hall Museum, Granite Dells, Thumb Butte, Bead Museum, Smoki Museum, Phippen Museum of Western Art

Yuma
Location: Southwestern corner
Year Founded: 1864
County Seat: Yuma
Major Cities: Yuma, Somerton, San Luis, Wellton
Square Miles: 5,509
Population: 110,750
Density: 18.1 Persons Per Square Mile
Major Industries: Farming, cattle, tourism, government, military
Attractions: Yuma Territorial Prison, Fort Yuma, US Quartermaster Depot, Quechan Indian Museum, St. Thomas Mission, Colorado River

Population Density: 1991 Department of Economic Security Projection.

Index

Bibliography

Annerino, John, *Outdoors in Arizona: A Guide to Hiking and Backpacking*, Arizona Highways, 1989.

Anthony John W., Sidney A. Williams, and Richard A. Bideaux, *Mineralogy of Arizona*, University of Arizona Press, 1982.

Arizona Department of Education, *Arizona Educational Directory*.

Arizona Department of Economic Security, *State Data Center Newsletter*.

Arizona State University, College of Business, Center for Business Research, *Arizona Business*.

Arizona Game and Fish Department, *Arizona Boating Guide*.

Community Development Program, Arizona Department of Commerce, *Arizona Community Profiles*.

Cook, James, *Arizona 101*, Cocinero Press, 1981.

Cook, James, Negri, Sam and Trimble, Marshall, *Travel Arizona The Back Roads*, Arizona Highways, 1989.

Arizona Department of Commerce, *Arizona's Changing Economy*, Commerce Press, 1986.

De Mente, Boye, *The Grand Canyon Answer Book*, Phoenix Books, 1989.

DeMente, Boye, *Arizona's Indian Reservations*, Phoenix Books, 1988.

Desert Botanical Gardens, *Arizona Highways Presents Desert Wildflowers*, Arizona Highways, 1988.

Eaton, Jerry, *The State We're In*, Southwest Publishing Company.

Granger, Byrd Howell, *Arizona's Names (X Marks the Spot)*, The Falconer Publishing Company, 1983.

Hirsch, Bob, *A Guide to Hunting and Fishing*, Arizona Highways, 1986.

Lehman, Charles A. *Desert Survival Handbook*, Primer Publishers, 1988.

Manning, Reg, *What Is Arizona Really Like?* Reganson Cartoon Books, 1968.

Maricopa Association of Governments, MAG *Regional Development Summary.*

Maricopa County Association of Governments, *Update of the Population and Socioeconomic Database for Maricopa County,* May 1987.

Office of Tourism, *Arizona Travel Planner*

Peterson, David A. and Hull, Andrew M., *Arizona Rental Rights,* Gem Guides Book Company, 1993.

Simpson, Bessie W. and Harry M., *Gem Trails of Arizona,* Gem Guides Book Company, 1984.

Statistical Abstract of the United States

Tegeler, Dorothy, *Destination: Phoenix,* Fiesta Books Inc., 1990.

Tegeler, Dorothy, *Retiring in Arizona,* Fiesta Books Inc., 1987, 1990.

Tegeler, Dorothy, *Moving to Arizona,* Fiesta Books Inc., 1988.

Tucker, Jack M. *Sun City.* Phoenix: Quail Run Books, 1985.

Tucson Economic Development Corp., *Tucson 1988 Enterprise Directory.*

Valley National Bank, *Arizona Statistical Review,* 1986-89.

Weir, Bill. *Arizona Traveler's Handbook,* Moon Publications, 1986.

Young, John V. *The State Parks of Arizona,* University of New Mexico Press, 1986.

Photo Credits

Bill McLemore, Cover

Department of Library, Archives and Public Records, State of Arizona, p. 21

Museum Division, Department of Library, Archives and Public Records, State of Arizona, p. 26

Office of Tourism, State of Arizona,
pp. 81, 89, 91, 95, 100, 132, 146, 153, 157, 177

Don Lilley, p.177

Dorothy Tegeler

Like most residents, Dorothy Tegeler lives in Arizona because it is the place she most wanted to call home. Her own experience relocating heavily influenced how this book was written. She's also written *Moving to Arizona*, *Destination: Phoenix*, a children's activity book, *Hello Arizona*, and co-authored *Arizona Favorites*.

An education graduate from Illinois State University, she has taught kindergarten through college. She has also handled employee communications for the Illinois Farm Bureau, and worked with Bobbs-Merrill and McKnight Publishing Companies in the Midwest.

Since arriving in Arizona in 1984, she has worked as an editor, researcher, writer, and ghostwriter. Her writing has appeared in *USA Today*, *Golf Digest*, *Advertising Age*, *Kiwanis*, *Communication World*, *Rotary* and *Medical World News*, as well as many local publications. Writing assignments have taken her inside many of Arizona's corporate headquarters, governmental offices, hospitals, schools, recreational facilities, magazines and newspapers.